the big black book

for parents

helping your teen navigate through life's challenges

the big black book

for parents

helping your teen navigate through life's challenges

by blaine bartel

Harrison House
Tulsa, Oklahoma

Unless otherwise indicated, all Scripture quotations are taken from the *King James Version* of the Bible.

09 08 07 06 05   10 9 8 7 6 5 4 3 2 1

the big black book for parents:
helping your teen navigate through life's challenges
ISBN 1-57794-722-3
Copyright © 2005 by Blaine Bartel
P.O. Box 691923
Tulsa, Oklahoma 74179

Published by Harrison House, Inc.
P.O. Box 35035
Tulsa, Oklahoma 74153

contents

contents (continued)

section two: helping your teen plan a fantastic future

contents (continued)

contents (continued)

contents (continued)

contents (continued)

contents (continued)

contents (continued)

section eight: what to do when your teen is almost done being a teen

contents (continued)

contents (continued)

dedication

To my Mum and Dad, Blake and Elaine Bartel. There are no words to describe all you mean to Luanne, Jason, and myself. If there was never another book written on parenting, the world could just pull up a seat and watch you.

introduction

I'm Blaine Bartel and I'm a parent of three teenagers. Oh yes, my incredibly brave wife, Cathy, has been my lifelong partner in this journey—this quest to magically transform these increasingly big children into responsible, deeply spiritual young adults. Neither of us asked for this job. You see, all we really wanted when this whole thing began was a baby or two, or three. Let me say very clearly for the record that we did not ask for teenagers. They just seemed to evolve before our very eyes.

Honestly, we didn't see it coming. One day it just happened. Our cute, cuddly, innocent yearlings soon turned into something that couldn't be tamed with some goofy pacifier or a warmed up bottle of milk. This was no quick fix. This teenager stuff was way different. It was going to take work, thinking, talking, planning, consulting, reading, praying, negotiating, understanding...and that got us through to age 14.

At first we weren't quite sure what to do. Being a full-time youth pastor, I was always telling parents what to do. That was my job. I was the expert. I knew all about teenagers. Come on, it couldn't be that hard. And besides that, I had parents. What they did raising me sure didn't seem that hard at the time. But everything changes when these little teenage tribal warriors are your own. They have your last name. And they are taking that name out into a wild teenage world. And as parents, you don't want the name to come home damaged, nor the bearers of the name. Something has to be done.

One colleague passed on a well thought-through plan when Jeremy, our first of three boys, turned 13. He told me, "Build a big wooden box. Put your 13-year-old in the box. Seal the box. Drill a small hole in the top of the box for air. When he turns 16...." I nodded curiously. "Plug the hole!"

Make no mistake. Raising teenagers may be the most difficult job you'll ever undertake. And it's a job you can't afford to quit. Quitting will levy a much heavier personal cost than the price you'll pay in the time, energy, love, and yes, even money you'll be required to expend to do the job right.

We've made our mistakes along the way. But Cathy and I have gladly given everything God and good parenting have asked for, and we have been justly rewarded. All three of our boys are serving God and living their lives to their fullest potential.

Jeremy has now graduated and is pursuing his dream in film making. Our middle son, Dillon, is a senior and is planning out his music career. Brock is a freshman and is going to play for the Dallas Cowboys. They all bear our name and we couldn't be more proud.

But it's taken work. And we still have a lot of it left to do. Important work. Big work. And that's why I'm happy to share with you our big black book. We've taken notes along the way. So read on. Your kids are worth it.

[SECTION ONE:]

[SECTION ONE:]

providing spiritual direction
to your teen

7 SURETIES OF GOD'S WILL FOR YOUR TEEN'S LIFE

Have you ever heard someone say, "God moves in mysterious ways"? I sure am glad that statement isn't true. The will of God doesn't have to be mysterious. Here are 7 things you can assure your son or daughter of that God has promised for their future.

1. God's will is salvation. Our heavenly Father desires that all of humankind have eternal life with Him. That includes your child.

2. God's will is dominion. Dominion simply means control. God wants your teen to apply His Word and take control of their body, thought life, attitude, and future.

3. God's will is discipleship. We are all to grow in our walk with Christ. As we mature, we are to help others do the same.

4. God's will is unity. Encourage your child's words and actions to be united with God's Word.

5. God's will is stewardship. Challenge them to take proper care of their time, money, abilities, and all God has entrusted them with.

6. God's will is relationships. Through the power of relationships, they will be able to accomplish things that would be impossible if they were on their own.

7. God's will is progressive. God has a plan for their life that will be completed one step at a time, not in leaps or bounds.

4 THINGS YOUR TEEN SHOULD LOOK FOR IN A MENTOR

A mentor is critical in the life of every successful person. Joshua had Moses. Elisha had Elijah. The disciples had Jesus. Oftentimes, mentors won't seek you out—we have to find them. Here are 4 clues in helping your teenager find the right one for them.

1.   A good track record. Look for someone who has a good history of success in the thing they want to do.

2.   Mutual benefit. Every great relationship will be good for both people. It is never one-sided. What can they do to help this potential mentor, bringing benefit to them?

3.   Unforced relationship. Allow the mentoring relationship to develop naturally. Don't try to force someone into this. Just find a way to be around this person by serving, helping, and contributing any way they can.

4.   Ask the right questions at the right time. Don't overwhelm this person to the point they want to avoid you. Be sensitive to the right opportunities to learn. Most of the time, they'll learn more by observing them.

7 SCRIPTURES TO GUIDE YOUR TEEN'S FUTURE

Can you imagine going into an uncharted forest without any map or compass? You might be lost for years. Many young people are living lost lives because they have thrown down the compass of the Word of God. Help them to memorize these Scriptures. Pray them over their future and let them guide all they do.

1. Jeremiah 29:11: "For I know the thoughts that I think toward you, says the Lord, thoughts of peace and not of evil, to give you a future and a hope."

2. Jeremiah 33:3: "Call to Me, and I will answer you, and show you great and mighty things, which you do not know."

3. Joshua 1:8: "This Book of the Law shall not depart from your mouth, but you shall meditate in it day and night, that you may observe to do according to all that is written in it. For then you will make your way prosperous, and then you will have good success."

4. Proverbs 18:16: "A man's gift makes room for him, and brings him before great men."

5. Ephesians 3:20: "Now to Him who is able to do exceedingly abundantly above all that we ask or think, according to the power that works in us."

6. 2 Timothy 1:9: "Who has saved us and called us with a holy calling, not according to our works, but according to His own purpose and grace which was given to us in Christ Jesus before time began."

7. Ephesians 5:15: "See then that you walk circumspectly, not as fools but as wise."

3 THINGS TO DO WHEN YOUR TEEN IS FEELING DOWN

Feelings come and go. We don't have the power to stop our kids from feeling discouragement, worry, or even depression. But we do have the power through Christ to give them the tools to overcome those feelings and move forward in life. Here's how.

1. Help them memorize 3 good Scriptures that they can quote out loud to themselves. Romans 10:17 says our faith comes on strong by hearing the Word of God! Three Scriptures I like to quote regularly with my boys are 1 John 4:4, Romans 8:31, and Ephesians 6 (putting on the armor of God).

2. Get them some inspirational music. Your child will have different music that inspires them and lifts their spirits, but I believe the very best is worship music because it is filled with the Word of God and helps their spirit commune directly with His.

3. Keep their mind and body active. Someone once said, "Idle time is the devil's workshop." One of the tools in that workshop is the thought of discouragement. When they're active, their mind is focused on the task at hand.

3 THOUGHTS TO ELIMINATE FROM YOUR TEEN'S THINKING

The Bible teaches us in 2 Corinthians 10:5 to cast down every high thought that would try to exalt itself against the knowledge of God. The act of casting down must be aggressive and then followed with replacement thoughts that encourage our walk with Christ. Challenge your son or daughter to guard carefully against these thoughts.

1. "No one cares about you." This temptation towards self-pity is a lie. People do care, and most importantly, God cares!

2. "You won't succeed." They have every reason to be confident if they are walking with God. Philippians 4:13 says you can do all things through Christ who strengthens you.

3. "Just give up." Jesus didn't quit on us. He doesn't have a quitting spirit, and He didn't put a quitting spirit in your teen. Encourage them to persevere and finish the race!

4 WAYS GOD GIVES YOUR TEEN DIRECTION

Your child is going to need clear direction in a number of areas in their life. And the good news is, God wants to give it to them. This direction is not hard to come by. Here are 4 ways He will give it to them.

1. **The Word (Bible):** the most practical way that God gives us direction. All other ways must line up with this way.

2. **Peace:** how God will lead us. His peace will be deep down inside letting your teen know they're headed in the right direction.

3. **People:** starting with you as a praying parent! And of course pastors, teachers, and spiritually mature friends as well. God will speak through people like these that He has strategically placed in their life.

4. **Desires:** what they really want to do. Maybe they like making art, building, or helping others. God has placed desires in their heart to help give them direction.

3 SECRETS TO KEEPING YOUR TEEN INSPIRED

Inspiration in our lives can come from a variety of places. God has a wonderful way of using different things to get our child moving in the right direction. Here are 3 secrets that have helped me inspire my teenagers in my day-to-day relationship with them.

1. The power of music. Although my sons will tell you that my radio is usually tuned in to sports-talk stations, I have learned to let music inspire me on a fairly regular basis. Whether it's a great new worship CD or just a song that stirs the soul, music has a unique way of lifting you up. I have encouraged my boys to let good music lift their hearts.

2. The power of a book. What you are doing right now is incredible. Congratulations! You are one of the few Americans that have taken time today to read a book. Of course, the Bible is different from all other books and should be in our regular reading, but other books also have the power to launch us forward. Put good books that relate well to your child in their hands as often as possible.

3. The power of people. The right people, that is. Like your teenager's youth pastor, or their good friends that push them to new heights in life. It might be a teacher, a coach, a brother or sister, anyone that can help them take new ground every day.

3 KEYS TO MOTIVATING YOUR TEEN TO DO DIFFICULT THINGS

The easy things come easy, don't they? It's easy to motivate your child to play their favorite sport, shop at their favorite store, or eat their favorite dessert. But how do we motivate them to do the hard things, like the day-to-day work at school or home, regular exercise, eating right, or any activity that you know they should be doing but everything inside of them says "no"? Here are 3 keys I've picked up along the way to motivate my kids.

1. Force them to start. There is something magical about "turning on the ignition key" and getting things going. It will give them that little bit of momentum to get rolling in the right direction. Make them start!

2. Help them keep the end result in mind. The Bible says in Proverbs 29:18 KJV, "Where there is no vision, the people perish." If you don't remind them why they're working, exercising, praying, reading, etc., it will become too easy to quit. Motivate them with a vision of what this activity is going to accomplish.

3. Reward them along the way. Create some kind of reward that you are going to give them for completing a task or activity. If might be watching their favorite show, getting a milkshake, going to a movie, or something else they like to do. God rewards us for doing right, so why can't we reward others!

4 SCRIPTURES TO PRAY OVER THE PLANS OF YOUR TEEN

I believe it is very important to pray the right things over the plans that we make. The Word of God tells us in Proverbs 16:9, "A man's heart plans his way, but the Lord directs his steps." We need to take the time to devise a plan, but as we pray God will direct each and every step to get there. Oftentimes these steps aren't even in our original plan set forth. Here are 4 Scriptures you can pray over all the plans your child makes.

1.   Mark 11:24: "Therefore I say to you, whatever things you ask when you pray, believe that you receive them, and you will have them." Believe that you receive your desired goal by faith.

2.   Psalm 37:4: "Delight yourself also in the Lord, and He shall give you the desires of your heart." Delight yourself In the Lord daily and your desires will be granted.

3.   Proverbs 21:5: "The plans of the diligent lead surely to plenty, but those of everyone who is hasty, surely to poverty." With diligent work your plan will make you rich.

4.   Galatians 6:9: "And let us not grow weary while doing good, for in due season we shall reap if we do not lose heart." Have a persevering spirit, knowing that you will reap if you don't give up.

4 WAYS THAT ANY TEEN CAN FIND FAVOR

Let's be honest. If we can get ourselves in favor with the most powerful Person in the universe, we're going to do really well. The great thing is that God has told us clearly in His Word that we can fall into favor with Him. Here are 5 ways to get your young person into supernatural favor with God.

1. He promises to reward and bless those who wholeheartedly seek Him. (Heb. 11:6.)

2. Searching out the wisdom of God's Word will bring good to them. He promises that when we discover His wisdom, we will obtain favor from Him. (Prov. 8:35.)

3. As they develop a lifestyle of praising God without apology, good things will happen. The churches in the book of Acts were bold to praise God with their voices and found favor with all the people. (Acts 2:47.)

4. Walking in goodness and integrity towards others will escalate their promotion. God promises us favor for our integrity but condemns the person who is wicked in one's actions. (Prov. 12:2.)

3 DAILY HABITS YOUR TEEN CAN DO TO GROW THEIR RELATIONSHIP WITH GOD

Habits make or break us. In fact, our lives are byproducts of the daily habits we form. Research has said it takes 21 days to form a habit. Take the next 3 weeks to help build these 3 habits in your teenager's life, and watch their walk with God grow.

1. At breakfast each morning, read one chapter of Proverbs. By the time they're done eating, they will have easily read a chapter.

2. Find one Scripture in the chapter they read that really stands out to them. Write it down on a piece of paper or a 3 x 5 index card and carry it with them wherever they go.

3. Whenever they hit slow times in their day, such as being stuck in traffic on the school bus, pull out the card and meditate on their Scripture.

As they commit to these 3 simple habits, they will grow rapidly.

3 THINGS THAT WON'T MAKE YOUR TEEN HAPPY

Happiness is not an act or an object. Happiness is not an event or goal that you eventually reach. True happiness is not a feeling that you can manufacture or a feeling that happens accidentally. Here are 3 things that the world tells teens will make them happy but always come up short.

1. Worldly fame. People who are in the spotlight are always smiling. It can even seem as though their lives are perfect. But being famous is no more a guarantee of happiness than being a car is a guarantee of being fast; it is what's under the hood that counts. There are undoubtedly happy famous people, and there is nothing wrong with being famous. More often than not, fame comes from being good at what we have chosen to do with our life. So encourage your child to pursue something they love, and they will be more likely to be good at what they do. Who knows, they might even become world famous. But if they pursue fame just to be famous, they will end up empty. (Ps. 1:2,3.)

2. Romantic love. Some of the most powerful emotions in life come from interacting with someone we have romantic feelings for. They can make us feel like the most important person on the planet. Then comes the inevitable—they let us down. The love of another human is never enough to fill a hole in your teenager's heart that is meant for a relationship with God.

Some young people search their whole lives for happiness because they attach it to the way people treat them. People will let them down, but God will always be there for them. Happiness comes from building a foundation in God and placing their relationship on that solid ground. (Matt. 7:24.)

3.   Much money. There is a saying that "money can't make you happy, but the things you can buy with it will." There is an undeniable thrill that comes from being able to buy something that we have always wanted. But that thrill quickly fades, and something else must take the place of the object we just bought. The circle doesn't end for young people who place all of their happiness in the stuff they purchase. The objects and the money are not bad at all, but expecting them to make us truly happy will leave us empty. God wants your child to have everything that they need, but they must honor God first and He will provide for all their needs, and happiness too. (Ps. 128:2.)

BO

[SECTION TWO:]

helping your teen plan
a fantastic future

3 WAYS TO HELP YOUR TEEN DISCOVER WHO THEY ARE

Perhaps one of the greatest journeys that your child will ever take is the one that leads them to the discovery of who God created them to be. They have a unique personality and skill set that God has entrusted them with. Many young people fail to realize all that God has made them to be. Here are 3 things to remember in assisting them in this exciting journey.

1. They will be incomplete without Christ. Maybe you recall the memorable scene in the Tom Cruise movie "Jerry McGuire," when Tom finds his wife whom he had separated from earlier and says to her, "You complete me." Just as God puts two people together in marriage, your son or daughter is to be married to Christ. Without that ongoing relationship with Jesus, they will always come up short.

2. They must study carefully what God has said about them. The Bible is full of Scriptures that describe the attributes and character that He has for them as a person. The Word of God is like a mirror. (James 1:23.) When they look at it and commit to do it, they take on the character of God.

3. Invite them to talk to you, as well as other family and friends, about their unique personality. Many times other people see things in us that we fail to recognize. They may be a great organizer, counselor, leader, giver, creator, or

helper and not even realize it until people around them recognize that ability in them.

4 WAYS TO HELP YOUR TEEN DISCOVER WHAT THEY CAN DO

Proverbs 18:16 promises, "A man's gift makes room for him, and brings him before great men." Believe it or not, God has put special gifts of ability in your child's life that you may not even be aware of yet. Here are 4 ways you can help them find out what all those gifts may be.

1. Seek God together in prayer times, asking Him to reveal their abilities. Jeremiah 33:3 tells us when we call upon Him, He'll show us things to come.

2. Ask people close to you. Solicit the evaluation of your spouse, friends, other parents, teachers, coaches, and those you trust to give their observations on your child's gifting.

3. Encourage them to try things they have in their heart. They should never be afraid to step out and attempt something they've never done.

4. They must faithfully do the little things they are asked to do, the things they don't like as much. God promises to give them bigger things when they do the small stuff well. (Matt. 25:23.)

3 THINGS THAT WILL MAKE YOUR TEEN BRILLIANT

Just because your teenager has a brain doesn't mean they are using it all that much. God has gifted them with a mind that they can learn to use and develop. Albert Einstein was a lifelong learner. If they learn to be a lifelong learner they will go far in life. The moment they stop learning is the day they begin a downward descent in life. Here are 3 qualities that will make them a great learner.

1. Teach them to ask questions. Science is simply the art of asking lots of questions and searching for the answer. What questions are they asking? When they are around people who know more than they do, encourage them to ask lots of questions. Then the trick is to shut up and listen.

2. Help them develop a teachable spirit. Someone once said, "It's what you learn after you know it all that counts." Some people limit their potential because they have an unteachable spirit. There isn't anyone who knows everything—except God (and last time I checked, your teenager wasn't Him). That means there's more for them to learn.

3. Challenge them to have passion. Great learners are passionate to grow. One time a student of philosophy asked his teacher how he could become a man of great wisdom. The teacher said, "Follow me and I will show you." The teacher waded into the ocean and the student followed him. The wise teacher then held his young pupil under water until the student began to

kick and fight his way to the surface. The student, gasping for air, asked, "What did you do that for?" The wise teacher replied, "When you want wisdom as much as you wanted air, you will find it."

Help them make a habit of never going to sleep without having learned something new that day.

4 SUREFIRE WAYS TO HELP YOUR TEEN FIND THEIR TALENTS

Proverbs 18:16 NKJV says, "A man's gift makes room for him, and brings him before great men." The discovery and implementation of your teenager's gifts and talents will bring them the success their heart desires.

Here are 4 ways you can help them to uncover their talents.

1. Ask those who work with your teen in sports, school, or hobbies what they see as your child's greatest qualities and assets. Sharing those things with your teen will help them to see that it's not just you who recognize their abilities.

2. Take time to pray together, and ask God to clearly reveal their gifts and talents. Jeremiah 33:3 promises that if we call on God, He'll show us hidden things which we don't know about.

3. Encourage them to follow the desires God has put in their heart, and dare to try new things. The results may surprise you.

4. Explain the importance of being faithful in little things they're asked to do, even if they aren't on their list of favorites. God tells us that if we're faithful in small things, we will be rulers over much. (Matt. 25:23.)

3 REASONS YOU MUST TEACH YOUR TEEN TO PLAN

Planning is one of the great secrets of success in any area of life. The great thing is this: The God we serve already knows how the future is going to look so He can help us plan better than anyone else. Sadly, there are too many teenagers who simply try to "wing it" in life. Here are 3 problems awaiting your child if you fail to teach them how to plan.

1. They will set up a life system for failure. You've probably heard the old saying, "Those who fail to plan, plan to fail." A lack of planning is actually a game plan to lose in life. Unprepared people are always unsuccessful people.

2. They'll never inspire others to follow them. People are afraid to walk in the dark. Ultimately, your child is going to want people to help them get where they want to go. When people fail to see a plan for where we are going to take them, they are most likely not going to sign up for the ride.

3. They'll give up more easily. A plan gives your teen the motivation they'll need to reach their goals by providing a definite finish line. A visual finish line helps give 100% towards getting to where they want to go.

3 KEYS TO TEACHING YOUR TEEN PLANNING SKILLS

If you want your child to succeed, you must help them plan for it. I am a huge hockey fan and player. Someone once asked my all-time favorite athlete, Wayne Gretzky, how he became the best goal-scorer in the history of hockey. He replied, "While everyone else is chasing the puck, I go to where the puck is going to be." He learned the value of planning ahead. Let's take a look at 3 keys to teaching your son or daughter to effectively plan.

1. Prayer. They may not know what the future holds, but they must believe that God does. God promises that as many as are led by the Spirit of God are the sons [and daughters] of God. (Rom. 8:14.) God will help your student to plan their day, their year, and their life as they become sensitive to the Lord in prayer.

2. Goal setting. Have your teenager write out exactly what they are currently planning for. You will be amazed how this key will begin to unlock their future.

3. Prioritizing. They will never keep their priorities if they don't have any. Putting things in order will help them to plan for and accomplish the most important things first.

4 STEPS TO HELP MAKE YOUR TEEN'S PLAN WORK

The Bible tells us in Psalm 37:23 that the steps of the righteous are ordered of the Lord. A good plan isn't accomplished in just 1 or 2 huge leaps that get us there quickly. It is going to take time and it is going to take multiple steps. Here are 4 steps that are necessary for your child's plans to become successful.

1. They should write down their goals. They cannot develop a plan when they haven't clearly established what they are trying to accomplish. It's got to be more than "I want a job." What kind of job do they want? What hours do they want to work? What kind of skills do they have? What work environment are they looking for? Write it down and teach them to be clear about their goals.

2. They must consult with people who have been where they want to go. This may involve taking someone to lunch or visiting them at their workplace. Perhaps they'll have to read a book or attend a seminar. Get all the information they can on their journey to achieve success.

3. They must put together the resources to make their plan happen. It may mean saving money, buying a weight set to train so they will make the football or soccer team, or simply writing down each resource and tool they'll need and figuring out what they are going to need to get them and use them.

4. Be realistic on the time line. We often try to bring our grandest plans to pass too quickly. Encourage them to give their plan the time it needs and not quit until they get there.

8 GOALS TO HELP YOUR TEEN REACH BEFORE THEY'RE 18

At every stage in life, it is important to learn to set incremental goals towards the fulfillment of your dreams and vision. I encourage you to challenge your child to write down their goals as a regular reference point for their progress. Here are 8 goals they should consider attaining before they're 18 years old.

1. Make a long-term financial investment in the stock market.

2. Read the Bible through entirely.

3. Hold down one job for at least 6 months—a year if possible.

4. Read Dale Carnegie's book *How to Win Friends and Influence People.*

5. Obtain a basic idea of what career direction they are going to take, and make the necessary plans for school or training.

6. Develop one strong friendship that they will keep for life, no matter where they both end up.

7. Save enough money to buy a decent used car.

8. Keep their grades up, and get their high school diploma.

3 KEYS TO FORECASTING YOUR TEEN'S FUTURE

Our plans are always an experiment with the future. A good plan that has any hope of being fulfilled must have accurate forecasting of the future. What field of work will be most valuable to your child and others in ten years? What is the next big idea in their area of expertise or interest going to be? If you'll follow these 3 keys, the Lord will help guide your son or daughter into a successful future others may find dim.

1. Teach them to spend time daily in prayer. It doesn't have to be long, as much as it should be consistent. Jeremiah 33:3 promises that if we call upon the Lord, He will answer us and show us things to come.

2. Remember that history repeats itself. A careful study of history will help us properly anticipate the future. In the early 1900s, people were calling for the U.S. Patent Office to be closed since everything had already been invented and it was unlikely anything new or helpful would come along! This was before airplanes, computers, television, and a million other things. The lesson of this piece of history is to never close your mind to the possibility of change that your child could take advantage of—in any area.

3. Two heads are better than one. I've found that I forecast better when I knock heads with my family, as well as my colleagues or coworkers. Challenge each other to dream and think outside the box called "today."

3 SMALL THINGS TO TEACH YOUR TEEN
THAT WILL CREATE BIG OPPORTUNITIES

Small things make a big difference. Just like we don't really think about windshield wipers or toilet paper until we need them or run out, the small things in life often get overlooked in the big picture of day-to-day living. Teaching your teenager to take the time to pay attention to these 3 small things may help them avoid pitfalls and create big opportunities.

1. Go the extra mile. People often miss great opportunities because they only do enough to get by. Teach your kids to make the choice to do the little extra things no matter how many people notice and do everything with excellence. Teach them to try to be the best at what they do, even if they are doing something that seems meaningless. Attention to detail and doing the little extras may be exactly what will open up a big opportunity.

2. Stay alert. Observation is one of the best tools to success. Even as they are faithfully doing what they know to do, teach them to keep their head up and looking around. Don't get so busy and robotic that they walk right past the greatest success. It may simply be a better way to do what they are already doing, but if they have their head buried in the sand, they will miss many wonderful opportunities.

3. Never quit. The only thing that happens when someone quits is to leave that much more victory for everyone else. The greatest achievements have come to those who have hung in the fight the longest. Opportunities are not created by sitting on the bench, so make sure your teen knows to make the choice to keep going, no matter what happens or how many times they get knocked down.

5 DECISIONS TEENS MAKE THAT SABOTAGE THEIR FUTURE

Who your teenager is now and who they will be is determined by the decisions they make. One out of every one person will make decisions. When we have to make a decision and don't, that is in itself a decision. So the question is what kind of decision-maker is your young person going to be? To help keep them from sabotaging their future, here are 5 bad decisions to warn them from making.

1. Disobedience to you as a parent. God has placed parents in the lives of teenagers to help guide them.

2. Make quick decisions. Before making a decision, they must learn to take time to think it over.

3. Develop wrong relationships. The people they spend time with will probably have the most influence on the decisions they make.

4. Wait for their big break. They must get off the couch and pursue their God-given destiny.

5. Give up. Both winners and losers face challenges, but winners don't quit.

4 THINGS TO TEACH YOUR TEEN ABOUT GOD'S LEADING

God has promised that He will lead and guide those who diligently follow Him. (Prov. 3:5,6.) There are times when you face a decision and you're not sure which way to go. When there doesn't seem to be a definite right answer, here are 4 questions your teenager should ask themselves.

1. "Do I have peace about it?" If they are born again, God has promised that the Holy Spirit will lead and guide them into all truth. (John 16:13.) James 3:17 says, "But the wisdom that is from above is first pure, then peaceable...." If it is not a question of right and wrong, the next step is to follow peace.

2. "Does it line up with God's Word?" God's Word is constant. (Ps. 119:89.) It is settled. So they will never get a leading that contradicts what God has said in His Word. The Bible is full of wisdom that will help them make good choices.

3. "Is it a step or a leap?" Psalm 37:23 says, "The steps of a good man are ordered by the Lord." God leads one step at a time. He will never ask them to do more than they are able. If it feels like a leap, it probably is. Take a step back and reevaluate the situation.

4. "Is it mutually beneficial?" God's kingdom operates on a system of exchange. Sowing and reaping, springtime and harvest, and labor and pay are all examples of exchange. God will not lead them to do something that requires them to sacrifice everything without compensation. Long-term, overseas missionaries, for example, have to make sacrifices in order to spread the gospel. But God will not ask your child to be a full-time missionary without also giving them ways and means to take care of themselves in exchange for being obedient. In Matthew 10:10, Jesus said, "A worker is worthy of his food." When God directs them to do something, there will be something beneficial that they will bring to the relationship and something good that they will take away.

[SECTION THREE:]

[SECTION THREE:]

**helping your teen find
favor in friendships**

5 QUESTIONS YOUR TEEN SHOULD ASK THEIR FRIENDS

A smart person is known by the good questions he or she asks. When Jesus was 12 years old, He was found in the temple asking questions of the teachers of the law. Teach your son or daughter to ask the right questions of their closest friends.

Here are 5 questions that good friends should ask each other.

1. How can I be a better friend to you?

2. Are there any traits, attitudes, or actions you see in my life that hinder my success?

3. What gifts and characteristics do you recognize as strengths in my life?

4. How can I pray for you at this time in your life?

5. What has God shown you in His Word lately?

5 WAYS TO HELP YOUR TEEN BE POPULAR
WITHOUT LOSING THEIR REPUTATION

Everyone wants to be popular. Popularity isn't a bad thing. In fact, Jesus was very popular during much of His ministry. He never compromised His character or morals to gain acceptance. You can encourage your teenager in their natural desire to become popular by making good choices and not bad ones.

Here are 5 roads to popularity your teen can travel without losing their integrity.

1. Be a kind person. They will never be short on friends.

2. When they do something, do it with all their might. Excellence draws a crowd.

3. Promote others and their accomplishments, not their own. God will then be able to exalt them.

4. Dare to dream big and pray for the seemingly impossible. People are drawn to those filled with hope and faith.

5. Stand up for what is right. Our world today is desperately searching for real heroes.

7 WORDS TO REMOVE FROM YOUR TEEN'S VOCABULARY

The Bible speaks about the power of words in relationship to our personal self-esteem. It says, "A wholesome tongue is a tree of life" (Prov. 15:4). Your child's words will bring life if they are good, but destruction if they are not. Here are 7 words you should help them to eliminate from their vocabulary right now.

1. *Can't.* You can do all things through Christ who strengthens you. (Phil. 4:13.)

2. *Never.* All things are possible to those who believe. (Mark 9:23.)

3. *Quit.* "Let us not grow weary while doing good, for in due season we shall reap if we do not lose heart" (Gal. 6:9 NKJV).

4. *Depressed.* "Rejoice in the Lord always: and again I say, Rejoice" (Phil. 4:4).

5. *Hate.* The Holy Ghost sheds the love of God abroad in our hearts. (Rom. 5:5.)

6. *Doubt.* "So then faith comes by hearing, and hearing by the Word of God" (Rom. 10:17 NKJV).

7. *Broke.* My God shall supply all of your needs by His riches in glory in Christ Jesus. (Phil. 4:19.)

4 FEARS YOU CAN HELP YOUR TEEN CONQUER EVERY DAY

Fear is the primary tactic of our enemy, the devil. All through the Bible, we are told to "fear not." Fear will immobilize your son or daughter, stopping them from reaching their goals and full potential. They will conquer their fears by studying, speaking, and acting on the Bible, God's Word. Remind them of this regularly and you will help them to conquer these 4 kinds of fear every day.

1. Fear of failure. This lie tells them that God is not strong enough to help them succeed, and it is perhaps the greatest attack of fear.

2. Fear of the future. This lie compels them to believe God is unable to see what lies ahead for their future and is not able to direct them in every step. (Ps. 37:23.)

3. Fear of the past. This haunting deception says that because of negative things that may have happened in times gone by, God is unable to make everything good today. (2 Cor. 5:17.)

4. Fear of comparison. This lie tries to talk them into believing God favors someone else more because that person appears to be doing better than they are. The enemy wants them to believe God has given up on them.

6 THINGS YOUR TEEN MUST BELIEVE ABOUT THEMSELVES

Your child will eventually become a product of what you and others teach them to believe. All great athletes, presidents, pastors, and corporate CEOs arrived where they are because they believed they could do something before anyone else believed in them.

Here are 6 things your teen must believe about themselves.

1. I have been given power over the devil. (1 John 4:4.)

2. I have been given power over every circumstance in my life. (Mark 11:23.)

3. I have a strong body that has been healed by the stripes taken on Jesus' back. (Matt. 8:17.)

4. I have the ability to control my mind and cast out evil thoughts. (2 Cor. 10:4,5.)

5. I am poised for success and will not accept any defeat as final. (1 Cor. 15:57.)

6. I hate sin but love all people and have favor everywhere I go. (Prov. 12:2.)

5 HABITS OF HAPPY TEENS

God wants your young person to be happy and enjoy life. That doesn't mean they will never experience trials or tough times. Here are 5 habits you can develop in your son or daughter that will cause them to keep their joy through even the darkest hours.

1. Regularly reading and meditating (thinking and pondering) on God's Word. (Ps. 119:105.) This will energize their joy!

2. Steadily communing with God. "Communion" comes from the word *communicate*. That's it! Encourage them to talk to God, praise Him, and give Him their requests and cares.

3. Vision thinking. Find out what God has gifted them in. Take time to seek Him for their career and ambitions. Help them take one step at a time as they grow to get there.

4. Singing a good song aloud! God made us to sing. Not all of us sound that good, but it doesn't matter. Find songs and worship music that inspire them for good. (Ps. 95:1.)

5. Attending church weekly. Being consistent in your local church will help them stay connected to good friends, strong mentors, and caring pastors who will help you keep them on track.

3 THINGS TO TELL YOUR TEEN ABOUT BEING COOL

Truly cool people don't have to work at it—they just are. Let's be honest: if you have to try to be cool, you probably won't have a lot of people looking up to you. Let's check out 3 reasons why cool doesn't have to try.

1. Being cool is an honor that only others can bestow upon you. Remember, the Bible's counterparts for the modern word *cool* are "favored and accepted." Only God and people can show you favor and acceptance.

2. Truly cool people focus on others, not on themselves. Matthew 23:12 says that those who humble themselves will be exalted.

3. Most cool people don't even realize they are cool. They're too busy making a difference in their world.

4 THINGS THAT YOUR TEEN SHOULD KNOW AREN'T COOL

I'm sure your young person has had someone at school try to impress them in some way. They were thinking, *Wow! Am I ever cool!* And they were probably thinking, *When is this person going to get a clue?* Once again, cool people don't have to work to impress you. Here are 4 things that are definitely not cool.

1.   You are not cool when you talk about yourself most of the time. The Bible says, "Let another man praise you, and not your own mouth" (Prov. 27:2 NKJV).

2.   You are not cool because of how you walk or what you wear. You are accepted and favored because of the good person you are, not the perception you try to create.

3.   It is definitely not cool to live a life of sin and personal pleasure. The Word of God warns us, "The way of transgressors is hard" (Prov. 13:15).

4.   It is not cool to make others feel small by putting them down with your words. Remember the law of sowing and reaping—if you sow encouragement, you'll reap it back.

5 THINGS THAT WILL STEAL FAVOR FROM YOUR TEEN

I want to help you with some important identification marks of young people who will not gain favor with others. The Bible is clear that there are certain behaviors in your teenager's life that will repel the blessings of God.

Here are 5 behaviors to encourage your teen to avoid.

1. If they constantly live in self-pity, looking to get attention, this is not cool.

2. If they try to impress people with their money, possessions, or accomplishments, they will lose favor.

3. If they are sharp-tongued, gossipy, and critical of others, another favor-buster.

4. If they only treat people they like and know with love and respect, not good.

5. If they spend the majority of the time thinking about themselves, having little regard for Christ and others, they will fall out of favor.

4 REASONS YOUR TEEN SHOULD WALK IN FAVOR WITH PEOPLE

God wants your son or daughter to be cool, accepted, and favored. The Scripture says, "Let not mercy and truth forsake you; bind them around your neck, write them on the tablet of your heart, and so find favor and high esteem in the sight of God and man" (Prov. 3:3,4 NKJV). You can enjoy favor, acceptance, and popularity with both God and people. Here are 4 reasons why you should be cool.

1. Favored, accepted people have the ability to influence others for good. That includes a witness of your Christian faith.

2. Favored people have confidence to do things others believe to be impossible or improbable.

3. Accepted people find it easy and natural to show others God's love and acceptance.

4. Favored people stand up for truth and don't need everyone to agree with them or even like them.

6 WAYS YOUR TEEN CAN BECOME A FAVOR MAGNET

Let's get right to the point: your teenager wants to be accepted and popular with people. Who doesn't? Now, you know they can't try to gain popularity and "coolness" the way the world tries to manufacture it. So how does a person become "Christ-like cool"?

1. They become cool when they stand up for what is right and don't care who stands with them.

2. They become cool when they reach out to the poor, the hurting, the lost—those who are "uncool."

3. They become cool when they take time for those many overlook—children. God loves kids, and so should we.

4. They become cool when they freely admit their shortcomings, pick up where they've failed, and move forward with godly confidence.

5. They become cool when they put God first in their words, their actions, and their plans.

6. They become cool when they couldn't care less about being cool.

4 STEPS TO HELP YOUR TEEN FIND FAVOR
WITH THEIR FRIENDS

Every teenager wants to have good friends. In order to have a good friend, they must learn to be one. There are very real reasons why everyone seems to like a certain person, while others are constantly rejected. Here are 4 practical steps you can help your teen to take in finding good friends.

1.   Break out of their shell of fear. They can't wait for people to reach out to them. They should be bold to say hello to people and make conversation.

2.   Give their friends some space. They shouldn't monopolize people's time or constantly follow them around. If they begin to smother people with attention, others will naturally want to avoid them.

3.   Be confident in themselves and their abilities. If they are constantly putting themselves down and wallowing in self-pity, people will tire of them soon.

4.   Have a giving heart without trying to "buy" their friendships. They should seek to be generous and thoughtful without feeling like they have to do things to keep a certain friend. If they have to buy or give someone something all the time, the person is probably not a friend anyway.

[SECTION FOUR:]

[SECTION FOUR:]

**protecting your teen
from dating dangers**

6 REASONS TO TEACH YOUR TEEN TO
SAY NO TO PREMARITAL SEX

The Bible teaches us in 1 Corinthians 6:18 to flee sexual immorality. God is not a "Grinch" trying to steal all the fun out of your son's or daughter's teenage years. He wants to protect them and prepare them for a wonderful marriage relationship where sexuality will have its perfect place.

It is your job as a parent to give them some concrete explanations that will provoke them to purity. Here are 6 reasons to teach them to say no.

1. They will keep the door closed on sin and its destructive nature.

2. The thought of raising a baby while they're a teenager will never have to enter their mind [or yours!].

3. They will never have a doctor tell them that they've contracted a sexually transmitted disease.

4. Friends and classmates will never see compromise in their life that will cause others to talk behind their back and lose respect for who they are.

5. God will be able to trust them with His very best as they give Him their very best.

6. They will never have to deal with "ghosts of relationships past" in their marriage relationship.

7 WAYS YOU CAN ARM YOUR TEEN TO FIGHT OFF PREMARITAL SEX

It's one thing to know that your teen should flee sexual immorality, but you may be wondering, "How do I help them to make the right choice not to do it?" Here are 7 ways that you can help them avoid the sin that can destroy them and their future.

1. Sexual sin starts in the mind, so challenge them to win the war there first by studying the Bible and other good Christian books. They must fill their mind with God's Word.

2. Stay in church. The more they hear the Word and stay close to other Christians, the better they will keep their focus on spiritual things.

3. Don't ever allow them to go out alone with a person you know will tempt them or easily give in to sexual sin. Stand your ground when you see trouble on the horizon!

4. Don't allow them to be alone with the opposite sex [even if it's someone you trust and like] in a place where temptation is easily fostered.

5. Teach them the importance of staying away from sexually suggestive books, magazines, photos, or Web sites that will only stir up sexual drive.

6.   Build a relationship of accountability with them and encourage them to do
     the same with other strong Christian friends. Let them know they can talk to
     you about anything and to simply ask for your help.

7.   Challenge them to make up their mind. Never retreat. Let every new friend
     they meet know they are committed to sexual purity.

6 SIGNS YOUR TEEN MAY NEED TO BREAK UP WITH SOMEONE

I have discouraged my teenagers from "going out" or "dating" too early. The Bible has much to say about developing good friendships but nothing about dating. As your teen grows older and a good friendship develops into a romantic relationship, be watchful to make sure things are on the right track.

And if they're not, step in and do something, before it's too late. Here are 6 reasons to encourage your teen to break off a relationship that has gotten off track.

1. If they are being pressured in any way to take the relationship to a "physical" level, it is inappropriate and a set up for disaster.

2. If they are verbally, mentally, or physically being abused in any way, get them out of the relationship—quickly.

3. If their partner doesn't show the spiritual drive and Christian attributes that you know are necessary to be strong for Christ, it's time to let go.

4. If they feel used in any way for what they have, give, own, or provide, they should stay out of the relationship. Be sure the person likes them because of who they are and what they stand for. Period.

5.   If you find the person they're with to be a liar, don't allow them to stick around. A real relationship can only be built on truth.

6.   If the person breaks up with them, let go. Seriously. There are many fish in the sea, and they may have just gotten rid of "Jaws," so encourage them to move on!

5 FRIENDS THAT WILL TAKE YOUR TEEN DOWN

The Bible tells us that those who walk with the wise will be wise, but the companion of fools will be destroyed. (Prov. 13:20.) Here are 5 different kinds of "friends" that can destroy your teen's relationship with the Lord. Help them avoid these kinds of people who will only bring hurt.

1. The mocker: the friend who always makes fun of spiritual things.

2. The doubter: the friend who believes and talks about the worst; usually the last to acknowledge what God can do.

3. The compromiser: the friend who goes to church and talks a good talk but, more often than not, does not back it up with a life that honors God.

4. The proud: the friend who thinks he or she is more spiritual than anyone else and constantly displays a critical attitude about everyone else's "lack of commitment."

5. The gossip: the friend who always "talks down" other people. If a person says negative things to them about his or her other friends, what is the person saying about them?

3 WAYS TO HELP YOUR TEEN FIND FAVOR
WITH THE OPPOSITE SEX

There is something that happens when your son or daughter moves into their teenage years. All of a sudden, they're not as concerned about "girls' germs" or "boys' germs" as they were when they were 7 or 8. During our teens, God slowly prepares us to someday enter into the covenant of marriage. It is important that they learn how to properly treat and respect the opposite sex, since they will eventually live with one of them forever. Here are 3 simple things to help your young person to remember.

1. Learn how to pass on sincere compliments about their character and accomplishments. Make them feel appreciated for who they are and what they've worked hard to achieve.

2. Be nice to all. Don't become "a snob" or "stuck up" by only associating with those who are good-looking or popular. Remember, Jesus died and shed His blood for every person, not just the ones He liked.

3. Show respect and purity physically. Their body belongs to them. Other people's bodies are not anybody else's property! The only time this changes is when 2 people are married. So, until that time comes for your teen, they must stay clear of tempting situations. (1 Cor. 7:1-4.)

6 THINGS TO TELL YOUR TEEN ABOUT FINDING A SPOUSE

Finding that special person God has for your teenager is one of the most important journeys they will take. Here are 6 things to help them in their search.

1. *Prepare.* Be sure they are ready emotionally and, most importantly, spiritually.

2. *Ask.* Pray for guidance in finding their spouse. Remember: we have not because we ask not. (James 4:2.)

3. *Obey.* Obedience to God's Word will keep them on the right track.

4. *Focus.* Keep their eyes and heart on Jesus, not the anxiety of searching.

5. *Wait.* They must be patient and understand that God has a perfect time for paths to cross.

6. *Relax.* As they are doing their part, God will take care of the rest.

3 THINGS TO TELL YOUR TEEN DATING IS NOT

Dating is not really a biblical word at all. That doesn't mean it's wrong to go out with someone on a "date." But it is important to remember what the Bible has to say about developing romantic friendships. If your teen is beginning to date without some clear guidelines and boundaries, they are headed for disaster.

Let's start by taking a quick glance at what dating is not.

1. Dating is not for those who aren't ready. In my opinion, dating shouldn't even be a consideration until a young person is at least 16 years old. That's been "the law" with my 3 teenage boys, and they're doing just fine with it. That doesn't mean they can't have good friendships with the opposite sex; just keep things in a group environment.

2. Dating is not a great way to "really get to know someone." Why? Because everyone is on their best behavior during a date. If they really want to get to know someone, watch the person at school every day, or both of them get a job together at McDonald's. Eight straight hours over a hot greaser full of fries will tell you the real tale.

3. Dating is not all it's cracked up to be. Think about 2 teenagers going out together who hardly know each other. They're young and have limited social skills. They have to try to create awkward conversation for hours on end.

The point is, it's usually a whole lot easier to get to know someone amongst a group of other friends who can help fill those awkward moments, keeping things fun.

3 WAYS CHRISTIAN DATING SHOULD BE DIFFERENT

The world's idea of dating is dangerous at best. That's why the Scripture tells us not to be conformed to this world, but to be transformed by the renewing of our minds. (Rom. 12:2.) We renew our minds with the knowledge of God's Word.

Here are 3 ways your teenager's Christian dating experience should be different from the way the world does it.

1. In the world, people date to check someone out; a Christian date is focused on building someone up. Dating in the world is like "trying someone on" like a pair of shoes—if they don't fit quite right for you, just disregard them and move on to someone else. A Christian's focus should be on encouraging each other in life and in one another's walk with God.

2. The world bases a large part of success in their dates on connecting physically, while Christians should be prizing spiritual things first. It's not that you shouldn't be attracted to someone by looks, but maintaining sexual purity must be at the top of your commitment to each other.

3. The world will often lie and deceive to achieve their goals in dating. Christians are to be committed to integrity and honesty. Tell your teen not to try to be someone they are not. Tell the truth. If someone doesn't like the "real you," don't worry about it. Obviously, that person isn't "the one."

3 THINGS EVERY STRONG CHRISTIAN GIRL WANTS IN A GUY

King Solomon said that a good man is 1 in 1000 and a good woman is nearly impossible to find. (Eccl. 7:28.) So if you have a son or sons, if they want to be that 1 in 1000, they can separate themselves from the pack by living up to these 3 magnetic characteristics.

1. A spirit of desire. Proverbs 21:25 says that the desire of a lazy man kills him. Girls are looking for young men who have vision, drive, and a desire for life and are willing to work to reach their goals.

2. A spirit of kindness. Proverbs 19:22 tells us that kindness is what is desired in a good man. Learning proper etiquette and manners in the way they treat people is important.

3. A spirit of justice. A just person is someone who has learned to distinguish right from wrong and is not afraid to stand up for truth. Don't allow them to back down to the pressure of friends to do wrong or compromise. Challenge them to have some backbone and be counted.

3 THINGS EVERY STRONG CHRISTIAN GUY WANTS IN A GIRL

All right, for those parents who have a daughter or two, turnabout is fair play. You have some expectations too. In a world that has become increasingly corrupt and vulgar, your daughter can stand above the crowd by the way she chooses to live. Anyone can follow the masses, but it will be the few who do the right thing who are exalted, promoted, and blessed with the best relationships and a bright future.

What does a good man want in a girl?

1. Devotion. A good man will chase a girl who chases after God and is unwilling to compromise and give in to the world. If your daughter is devoted to Christ and devoted to His plans for her life, guys will follow!

2. Wisdom. Knowledge is the acquiring of facts and information. Wisdom knows what direction to go with those facts and information. Guys search for a young woman who has the ability to discern and make good decisions.

3. Encouragement. Throughout the Bible, we are instructed to encourage one another, inspiring others with our words and good works. We must learn to build people up, not tear them down. A man needs a woman who believes in him and will be a regular source of strength and encouragement.

4 SIGNS A RELATIONSHIP IS LUST-CENTERED

Here are some signs you can look for in your teenager's relationships to see if they have strayed from God's kind of love to fleshly lust.

1. An unhealthy obsession with looking at the opposite sex. (Matt. 5:28.) This doesn't mean they can't look at the opposite sex in a decent manner, but encourage them to guard against looking with impure thoughts.

2. A willingness to compromise eternal rewards for short-term physical contact and pleasure. (Heb. 12:16.) Encourage them to take the path Moses did. He forsook the sinful pleasures of Egypt for the eternal reward from God. (Heb. 11:24,25.) The pleasure of sin lasts only for a season, but the reward of purity lasts forever.

3. Manipulating others to get what they want. "Baby, if you really loved me, you would prove it." If they really loved the person they said that to, they wouldn't ask him or her to compromise God's Word. The proof of love isn't physical; it's obeying God's Word and keeping Him at the center of their relationships.

4. The feeling they may have to give in to the other person's pressure because they are afraid he or she won't love them if they don't. Perfect love casts out all fear. (1 John 4:18.) If their love is based on God's Word, they won't fear a

human being. They will be more concerned about what God thinks than what anybody else thinks.

5 STANDARDS TO SET FOR BEING THE RIGHT PERSON

Start by asking your son or daughter some questions. Are you the right person? Are you the man for the job? Are you the woman who will not compromise? We all want that right job, car, spouse, future, or opportunity. For those things to come our way, each of us must first be the right person.

They can begin now to develop these 5 characteristics of the right person.

1. Integrity is one of the most important characteristics that anyone could have. The right person is the same no matter whom one is with, what one is doing, or where one is. Image is not everything; integrity is. In the end, their life is about being, not appearing.

2. The second key characteristic of the right person is humility. Proverbs 16:18 NIV says, "Pride goes before destruction, a haughty spirit before a fall." They cannot live a life of destruction and expect to be or find the right person.

3. Everyone should have an ongoing desire to grow, no matter if it's to get good grades, find a spouse, or receive a promotion. A desire to grow will help them get there. Keep in mind that the proof of a desire to grow is the pursuit of that desire.

4. Self-control is the fourth key characteristic of the right person. The right person has an understanding that he or she cannot do everything they "feel" like doing. If it were up to most of us, we wouldn't even get out of bed half the time. As they are on that road to becoming the right person, they must gain control of what they do.

5. The last characteristic is friendliness. It almost sounds too easy, but this characteristic will take your child a long way. No one wants to be around unfriendly people. Think about it. If you went to a restaurant and the food was good but your server was a rude, unfriendly jerk, you would probably think twice before making this the "right" restaurant. Remind them to keep in mind the importance of being a friendly person.

[SECTION FIVE:]

OPEN

[SECTION FIVE:]

critical things to tell
your teen about money

6 STEPS TO HELPING YOUR TEEN FIND FAVOR IN THEIR WORK

God wants to help your young person succeed in all their work. Their success in their job and career will be a direct result of their ability to get along with people. One of the most fulfilling things in the world is having a job you love and working with people you really like. Here are 6 steps to help get your teen there.

1.   Don't treat their boss one way and everyone else a different way. People will see hypocrisy and resent them.

2.   Never cheat their company or business by stealing. I'm not just talking about their products or supplies; this also includes their time. If they're con-stantly late to work, taking long breaks, or leaving early, it's like stealing money out of the cash register, because "Time is money."

3.   Don't try to destroy someone at their work in order to get that person's position for themselves. It will eventually backfire, and they'll reap what they've sown!

4.   When someone else does a good job at their work, compliment the person personally and in front of their boss.

5.   Never try to take authority or leadership that hasn't been given to them. Just do their job, and stay out of business that isn't theirs.

6. Always give 100 percent. If they can give 110 percent, they were never giving 100 percent in the first place!

5 SCRIPTURES TO PASS ON TO YOUR TEEN ON GIVING

Every day your teenager will have a choice whether to give or not to give. Whether it's their little brother who wants to borrow something or a crazy friend who wants them to shave his head bald, here for their encouragement are 5 Scriptures on giving.

1. Luke 6:38: Giving not only blesses the receiver, but also the giver.

2. Proverbs 21:26: As the righteousness of God, we are not to be stingy in our giving.

3. 2 Corinthians 9:7: Be sure your heart is in the right place while giving.

4. Matthew 10:8: God has blessed us so that we may bless others.

5. Acts 20:35: The giver is better off than the one who receives.

3 REASONS GIVING FAMILIES FIND UNUSUAL FAVOR

Favor can bring you before the right people and set up the right circumstances. Wouldn't you like to have favor? Wouldn't it be great if your young person grew up understanding the principle of favor and how to aquire it? Why not start developing a giving family? If you're still not convinced, here's why:

1. It's a spiritual law. As you give, it is as if you are making deposits into a favor bank account that you can withdraw at any time. (Luke 6:38.)

2. People like givers. As you give, you become a giant magnet for unusual favor. Don't you enjoy being around givers? I thought so.

3. God is on your side. As you are obedient to God's Word, God will open up doors of favor in your life.

5 WAYS MONEY CAN DESTROY YOUR FAMILY

Movies, and most other media, paint the picture that money is the solution to all your problems. "If you have more money, everything will be better." That is not true. In fact, money, if handled and perceived incorrectly, can destroy people. Here are 5 ways money can destroy, if not handled with wisdom and integrity.

1. Money can give a false sense of security. Jesus rebuked the church of Laodicea in Revelation 3:17 because they were cold toward Him, thinking they were okay because they had wealth.

2. Money can cause people to worry about a need for more. Jesus said that our lives do not consist in the abundance of our possessions. (Luke 12:15.)

3. Some people in their greed for more money will compromise to gain. What they compromise to gain, they will have to compromise to keep; but they will eventually lose it all. (Prov. 13:11.)

4. When people have money, they often worry about losing it. The money they thought would give peace of mind now enslaves them to fear.

5. Love of money can choke God's Word from being fruitful in our lives. (Matt. 13:22.)

Money isn't a bad thing. In fact, it can prove to be a powerful tool for good in the hands of the right person. Make sure your family isn't destroyed by the 5 misconceptions of money.

3 REASONS WHY YOUR TEEN IS MORE IMPORTANT THAN YOUR MONEY

It's sad, but some people find out too late in life that their kids are more important than money. They spend their whole lives pursuing an inanimate object that can't live, love, or laugh. In their passionate pursuit, they ignore and neglect their loved ones. When they grow old, they find themselves wealthy but alone. None of their kids or grandkids visit them. Their spouses, tired of neglect, have left them.

Don't get to the end of your life and find yourself all alone. Money is a poor comfort. Here are 3 reasons your family is more important than money.

1. You can take people with you to heaven, but your money stays here. People are eternal spirits whom you can lead to Christ and spend eternity with. Money wastes away.

2. People will love you, but money cannot. You can't buy love, and money can't replace the fulfillment that comes from being loved by people.

3. People can comfort you when you're ill, but money can only buy doctors. Friends can encourage you and laugh and cry with you, and they won't bill you for it.

Don't neglect the important relationships in your life for money, or you might one day find yourself alone.

4 PRIORITY CHECKUPS TO GIVE YOUR TEEN

Take this little test with your teen to see if they are balanced in their views of money.

		YES	NO
1.	When you're undercharged $20 at the store, do you return the extra money?	❏	❏
2.	You see someone drop their wallet. You open it to find $500 cash. Do you quickly flag the person down to return it?	❏	❏
3.	When you receive any money, do you always set 10 percent aside for God? Are you excited to bring it to church and give Him your tithes?	❏	❏
4.	You see a friend in a financial crisis and you feel a prompt in your heart to give him or her your last $25. Do you do it?	❏	❏

Total your "yes" and "no" answers and rate how you handle money. Four "yes" answers: you're doing great. Three "yes" answers: you are on your way to financial greatness—keep improving. Two "yes" answers: your character with money is weak;

your financial future isn't looking too bright. One "yes" answer: keep your day job; you're taking a tough financial road. Zero "yes" answers: you're a scrooge and on a highway to poverty.

6 "REAL LOVE" ATTRIBUTES YOUR TEEN NEEDS TO SEE IN YOU

You can't buy love, and you can't replace love with money. What many people call love is really just an emotion they are feeling at the moment. Read 1 Corinthians 13 to discover the true definition of love. Here is a quick summary of 6 attributes of real love.

1. Love gives with no strings attached. Some people give nice gifts but attach strings. Real love gives expecting nothing in return.

2. Love looks for what it can give rather than what it can get. This perspective would change 99 percent of American relationships. Do you see people as opportunities to gain something for yourself or as an opportunity to give?

3. Love is quick to forgive. It doesn't keep a running tab of past offenses. Freely God has forgiven us; freely we should forgive others. (Matt. 10:8.)

4. Love is patient. This is tough in today's "must-have-it-now," drive-up-window society. But love is patient with others because God is patient with us.

5. Love has a humble heart and attitude. Real love knows that anything good we have is because of God's goodness in our lives. We can't take the credit. It all belongs to God.

6. Love is respectful and courteous of others.

3 REASONS TO MODEL TITHING FOR YOUR TEEN

There are really more than 3 reasons you should tithe; but if these don't inspire you to tithe, another 100 reasons won't either.

1. God said if you don't, you're robbing Him. (Mal. 3:10,11.) This doesn't sound like a very good plan. I'm sure God has a good security system that lets Him know anytime a thief robs Him of His tithes. Do you think God is going to bless a thief who is robbing Him?

2. God said that if you do what He says, He will flood you with blessings. It sounds like a good thing to be flooded with blessings. What a great testimony the blessings of God are to your teen when they understand that tithing is what opens the windows!

3. God will work His pest control on anything that will try to attack your finances. Some people lose great financial crops because of pests, accidents, theft, and so forth. The Bible promises that the devourer will be stopped in the life of a tither.

God says, "Test me in this" (Mal. 3:10 NIV). Put Him to the test. Honor Him with your tithes, and you will be passing on to your teen one of the greatest examples of obedience you could give them.

4 WARNINGS JESUS GAVE ABOUT MONEY THAT ARE WORTH PASSING ON TO YOUR TEEN

Jesus taught many things about money. In His teachings, He shared the heavenly Father's plan for provision and prosperity, but He also gave some very stern warnings. Four warnings He gave are also important for us and our young people today. Passing these on to your son or daughter will help them avoid many problems.

1. Matthew 6:19 NIV: "Do not store up for yourselves treasures on earth, where moth and rust destroy, and where thieves break in and steal." This doesn't mean we don't save money, but rather that we don't put all our hope in money here. We should be wise and give generously to His kingdom, and we will have riches in heaven as well.

2. Matthew 6:24 NIV: "No one can serve two masters. Either he will hate the one and love the other, or he will be devoted to the one and despise the other. You cannot serve both God and money." You must choose whom your focus will be on—God or money. You can't be devoted to both.

3. Matthew 6:25 NIV: "Therefore I tell you, do not worry about your life...." Worry robs us of joy, faith, and time. It never produces good fruit. Trust God to provide for you.

4. Matthew 13:22 tells us not to let the deceitfulness of wealth choke out our love for God and His Word.

As your teen takes heed to these warnings, they can expect great success.

7 REWARDS OF THE GIVING TEEN

If your teenager has unsaved friends that think they get the short end of the deal by being a giver, tell them to think again. Take a look at these 7 rewards Scripture promises to your child as they are obedient to give.

1. They will prosper. (Prov. 1:25.) That's much better than the alternative.

2. They will be refreshed and encouraged by other people. (Prov. 11:25.) We all need this at different points in our lives.

3. They will get back what they give, but it will come back bigger and better. (Luke 6:38.)

4. God personally sees to it that they receive their reward. (Eph. 6:8.)

5. They will be flooded with good things. (Mal. 3:10.)

6. They will have supernatural protection over their money and possessions. (Mal. 3:11.)

7. They will have treasure in heaven that no one can take away. (Luke 18:22.)

Encourage them to take advantage of the rewards available to them by being a giver. They can watch others be blessed, or they can obey God's Word and receive blessings too.

3 BIBLE PERSONALITIES TO INTRODUCE TO YOUR TEEN

We often have the wrong idea that if we are going to sell out to Jesus, we must brace ourselves for a life of poverty. However, the opposite is true. When you see people in the Bible who surrendered their lives to God, you see them richly blessed beyond their wildest expectations. It is important that your young person sees that God blessed His people throughout the Word of God.

1.   Abraham obeyed God and left his homeland of Ur to follow God. He became very wealthy in livestock, silver, and gold. (Gen. 13:2.) He also became a great nation. (Gen. 12:2.)

2.   Solomon, King David's son, chose to follow God at a very young age and asked God for wisdom. God was pleased with his request and gave him wisdom and great riches. (1 Kings 3:10-13.) His palace took 13 years to build; it was a beautiful home. (1 Kings 7.) People came from all over the world to see Solomon's wealth and hear his wisdom. (1 Kings 10.)

3.   Contrary to popular belief, Jesus was financially blessed. He had a full-time staff of 12 He took care of. He had an accountant named Judas (not a really honest one) to handle the money. We know He dressed nicely because Roman soldiers gambled over His clothes at the cross.

As we obey God and follow His Word, we can be financially prosperous, no matter how old or how young we may be.

3 THINGS YOUR TEEN SHOULD KNOW ABOUT
BEING GOD'S CHANNEL

Webster's dictionary defines a channel as "the course that anything moves through or past."[1] If your teen is willing to become a channel, God will be able to trust them with wealth and possessions. Too many Christians become wells instead of channels, holding on to what they get, refusing to allow their blessings to flow to others. So here are 3 reasons God is looking for them to be His channel.

1. As a channel for blessings, they will reflect God's character. God's very essence is to give. John 3:16 says that He so loved that He gave. When they give is when they are most like God.

2. As a channel, they will see no limit to what God can bring their way. When the Lord knows He can trust them to obey Him with all their provision, they are unlimited in their potential.

3. A channel is always left with the residue of whatever comes through it. Even as they obey God in giving, He will see that they continue to be blessed in the process.

NO
ENTRY

[SECTION SIX:]

[SECTION SIX:]

how to help your teen win respect with authority, including you

7 THINGS CONSISTENT PARENTS CAN
LOOK FORWARD TO IN THEIR TEEN

The Bible tells us that a wise child will make one's father happy, but a foolish child will cause one's mother grief. (Prov. 10:1.) The attitudes and actions your child displays in your home will cause you either happiness or heartache. Parents who invest time in lovingly correcting and disciplining their teenager consistently can look forward to this rewarding behavior.

1.   They will actually learn to do their chores without someone asking them to do them.

2.   They may even offer to help with something around the house that is not usually their responsibility.

3.   They will give you a compliment with no hidden agenda.

4.   They will ask you if there is anything they can do to make things better in your home.

5.   When asked to do something, they won't procrastinate.

6.   If they have a brother or sister, they will treat their sibling with the same respect that they would want in return.

7. They will be polite, thoughtful, and helpful outside of the home, at school, and in other activities.

3 SECRETS TO TEACH YOUR TEEN
ABOUT BEING A GOOD LISTENER

The Bible says in James 1:19 NIV that we are to "be quick to listen, slow to speak." Unfortunately, many people are just the opposite and are very quick to speak and extremely slow to listen. When you take the time to listen to somebody, you are showing them that you care and have respect for what they think. It will cement your relationship with that person. What does it take to be a good listener? Here are 3 secrets that every parent should share with their teen about being a good listener.

1. Look into the eyes of the person you are listening to. This, more than any-thing, says, "I really do care about what you have to say."

2. Think about the point or concern they are making. Don't be rehearsing in your mind your answer before you've fully caught all that they are communicating.

3. Repeat back a brief synopsis of what they just told you. For example, "Jim, I understand that you want to borrow $150 from me, but number one, I'm not a bank, and number two, I don't have an extra $150."

5 REGRETS YOUR TEEN SHOULD NEVER LIVE WITH

Providing guidance and correction will be a key in helping your teenager get the best out of their life. The world is full of people who look back with regret on their teenage years. They longingly wish they had done things differently. You have the opportunity right now to help them live life without regrets.

Here are 5 regrets you want to discourage them from ever having the rest of their life.

1. Moral regrets. Compromising their purity will result in the memories and stains of sexual sin. (Rom. 12:1.)

2. Ministry regrets. If the Lord is speaking to them about sharing their faith with a classmate, tell them to take the opportunity. It may never come again.

3. Mentor regrets. Submit to a good youth pastor and others they trust to mold them and develop them as a leader. Now is their greatest time of learning and personal development.

4. Maximum regrets. Never leave wondering what could have happened—in school, athletics, church, or any other part of life—if they would have given all they had to give to succeed.

5. Media regrets. Don't ever look back at their youth as a time when all they did was watch TV, play video games, and go to movies. Do something productive in life, along with entertainment.

7 QUESTIONS TO ASK YOUR TEENAGER IN THE NEXT 7 DAYS

Asking questions is a great way to learn and grow as a parent trying to lead their teenager. You gain a perspective on areas of your life that you may have never realized. Here are 7 questions to ask your teenager in the next 7 days.

1. How can I be a better parent to you?

2. What do you see as my greatest strengths in giving you love and guidance?

3. What do you think are some things I could do better?

4. What friends do you see as the best influences in your life?

5. What kind of career could you see yourself getting into after you graduate?

6. When do you feel most proud?

7. What is the most important thing you've learned in life so far?

6 THINGS YOUR TEEN SHOULD KNOW
BEFORE THEY BREAK THE LAW

The Bible says in Romans 13:1-2 that every person should be subject to a governing authority and that our resisting that authority will bring judgment on us. Here are 6 things your young person should know if they choose to break the law, whether it is exceeding a speed limit or taking something that belongs to someone else.

1.   God is bound by His Word to back up those who establish the laws, not you.

2.   Even if you are not caught immediately, the consequences will eventually catch up with you.

3.   Know what living on the inside of a 4' x 6' prison cell feels like, because that will be your future home.

4.   Go down to the local jail and meet the criminals. If you choose to break the law, they could be your best friends.

5.   Get a job making 50 cents an hour. That's about what they'll pay you in prison.

6.   Realize that smaller violations will slowly but surely lead you to larger ones. It will become a downward spiral that is difficult to recover from.

3 WAYS TO ENCOURAGE YOUR TEEN TO FIND FAVOR WITH YOU

One of the best things in life is enjoying a happy home. Your teen can learn to become ones of the great sources of joy in your family. I've got 3 teenage boys who everyone at school and church thinks are really "cool." But they are also great guys at home. The rebel attitude will not bring them blessing. In fact, it will cause them some very bad moments in their life. Here are 3 things you can pass on to ensure them a great time at home.

1. "Choose to obey your parents immediately, whether you feel like it or not." They're eventually going to have to do it—right? So they should just get it done and out of the way.

2. "Honor your parents when you speak to them." Even if they don't agree with you and want to discuss something or negotiate a "better deal," tell them to do it without the anger and the attitude. They'll be amazed at the results!

3. "Be truthful, even when it gets you in trouble." They lose favor quickly when they cannot be trusted. It is better to take the heat if they have it coming, than to lie and avoid it. Lies are eventually uncovered, and the conse-quences are much more damaging than telling the truth would have been.

3 WAYS PARENTS WILL AFFECT THEIR TEEN'S CAREER

Your relationship with your teen is simply preparation for the rest of their life, including their work and career. There are at least 3 important reasons their career will either succeed or fail as a direct result of how they get along with you. It would be good to remind them of this regularly.

1. If they can't honor and obey those who love them in their home, it's unlikely they'll behave any better with a boss who won't be nearly as likely to forgive. Parents will be the last bosses they have who can't fire them.

2. You have already been where they are headed. You have experienced the real world. If they're smart, they'll ask questions, listen to your experiences and wisdom, and learn what it takes to succeed.

3. There will be times when school, chores, and life at home will seem boring and redundant. The day will come when they will experience the same feelings with their job and career. Learning to persevere and rejuvenate their passion will put them ahead of the pack.

4 WAYS ANY PARENT CAN ALLOW THEIR TEEN
TO BECOME SELFISH

Have you ever wondered how your own teenager could be so selfish? To answer that question and to help them avoid this pitfall in the days ahead, here is a list of 4 reasons why parents can allow their kids to become selfish.

1. They make the choice to let them make selfish decisions. We must teach them to make a decision not to be selfish, even if they don't feel like it. I have found that as we act on a right decision, the feelings will come.

2. They haven't allowed their teen to experience firsthand the joy of giving. Not only will an unselfish act bring joy to others, but the giver will receive joy as well. Give them a chance to share that!

3. They have not encouraged their son or daughter to renew their thinking. We're all born naturally selfish, but that doesn't mean we must stay that way. We need to teach our kids to put selfless thoughts in and selfish thoughts out.

4. They're letting their teens act unthankful. Unthankfulness will cause people to become selfish. People who are unthankful stop recognizing the goodness of others; therefore, they develop an unwillingness to give.

6 ACTIONS EVERY PARENT SHOULD MODEL FOR THEIR TEEN

God is love, and as imitators of Christ we are to illuminate His love towards others, especially our kids. Maybe you need some advice to get started. Here are some potential actions to get the ball rolling. Trust me, your teen will watch and learn!

1. Be polite. Treat others with respect. Say please and thank you. Also remember, dads: ladies first.

2. Smile. Show off those pearly whites. This small gesture will go a long way.

3. Share. This unselfish act is packed with power.

4. Listen. Give others your full attention. They will appreciate the investment.

5. Lend a hand. Mow the lawn for an elderly neighbor, or send a card to a relative you have been praying for.

6. Give a gift. There doesn't have to be a special reason, but the best reason of all is to simply say, "I care about you."

3 SACRIFICES THAT WILL BRING YOUR TEEN
THE FREEDOM THEY WANT

You can get a lot of things for free in life. Those AOL CDs at the grocery store. Mints at a restaurant. Real estate booklets at the convenience store. But one thing I can promise you is not free are the freedoms every teenager desires. They must work and make sacrifices to gain new freedoms. This is true in the way they treat you as parents, their work career, or any other area of life. Here are 3 sacrifices they should be taught to make to gain future freedom.

1. The sacrifice of honesty. Even when it hurts, honesty must be a value they hold true to. When they develop a reputation for always being honest, even when it's to their detriment, people will trust them with freedoms not afforded to others.

2. The sacrifice of diligence. When you see them doing their homework, yard work, chores, or a part-time job well and without complaints, their freedoms will rise.

3. The sacrifice of servanthood. Rather than demanding their rights, start serving others' requests. When they develop a heart that is "others first," others will start to put "them first."

3 THINGS YOUR TEEN MUST TELL YOU

Communication is the key to victory in any kind of relationship. Great companies, great armies, great churches, great sports teams, and great homes all have one thing in common: They have learned to communicate effectively with one another. Communication is not talking. It is listening, observing, studying, and finally, talking. Young people who only learn to talk are not communicating; they are spewing. In opening up good communication lines with your son or daughter, here are 3 things they must always commit to tell you.

1. Tell you when they need help. It may be in school, a relationship, or a job, but if they need help and guidance, let you know. That's why God gave you to them—to help them get through tough times.

2. Tell you when they've made a mistake. It might be easier at the time to try to cover it up, but honesty will not only help them to not make this same mistake again, it will also earn them big points in the "trust" quest.

3. Tell you they love you. (They should be hearing this from you first!) Sure, there's no such thing as a perfect parent, but they're not perfect either and you love them anyway. Communicating out loud your love for one another is important for a strong relationship.

3 THINGS YOUR TEEN NEEDS TO KNOW
ABOUT A COMMANDMENT

This whole "rules" thing got started a long time ago with Almighty God. Moses came down from a mountain with 10 commandments from God. When lived by, the children of Israel had great victory. When forgotten, they suffered horrendous defeats at the hands of their enemies. But there is more to God's commandments than meets the eye. Let's look at the commandment "Thou shalt not steal" and see 3 keys to every rule God has given to your young person.

1. We must know the Person behind the commandment. If God tells us not to steal, then we can trust Him as an important Person in our world not to steal from us. He won't break His own commandment. Your teen can trust God. He's on their side!

2. We must know the principle behind the commandment. The principle He wants us to learn from "Thou shalt not steal" is respect. If they respect someone, they won't take what belongs to him. If they fail to respect others, they will quickly lose respect as well.

3. We must know the power behind the commandment. If God asks us to abide by one of His guidelines for living, He is obligated to provide the ability to live it out. That's why it's important to stay in relationship with God through

His Son, Jesus. God promises to work in them to perform His will and pleasure. (Phil. 2:13.)

[SECTION SEVEN:]

[SECTION SEVEN:]

developing discipline and
work ethic in your teen

3 REASONS WORKING AT HOME WILL
TAKE YOUR TEEN TO THE TOP

Has your teen ever asked, "What do I get out of this?" If so, tell them you're glad they asked. Maybe they get an allowance you can point to as some form of payment for their help with the family chores. But maybe not. We've never had a regular allowance with any of our teenagers, but they've always worked very willingly because they care about our family and understand that rewards will come. So here are 3 ways helping out Mom and Dad will help them even more.

1. Family life is training camp for life's big leagues. I'm so glad now that my parents instilled great work habits in me when I was a teenager. They gave me all that I would need to make my bosses happy and get me many raises along the way.

2. They are sowing seed that will harvest in their own home one day. I believe one of the reasons my 3 boys have always been good workers in our home is that I was a good worker in my house. The Bible says in Galatians that God is never mocked and that anytime a seed of any kind is sown, you will reap in due season.

3. Helping Mom and Dad gives them favor. It won't be long until they really need something from you. Every willing, well-done work puts another good

deposit in their favor account with you. Withdrawals are easier when they've put something in the bank.

6 WAYS YOUR TEEN WILL BE PROMOTED BY THEIR BOSS

No one likes to work at a job without being recognized and even promoted for one's labor. Especially a teenager. They want to know their work is accomplishing something. And they want to be recognized for what they do. There are reasons why some people seem to climb the ladder of promotion and authority, while others remain on the lowest rung. Here are 6 ways your teen can see promotion at work.

1. Encourage them to always arrive a few minutes early for work and then to stay at least a few minutes late.

2. Do not allow personal issues or other relationships at their job to take time or focus away from their work.

3. Tell them to never complain about their pay. They agreed to work for that amount, so they ought to be grateful!

4. They should ask their boss from time to time if there is anything they can do to improve their performance.

5. Show them how to work with their head, not just their hands. Help them think of ways to do their job more effectively.

6. Don't let them continually badger their boss with requests for promotions or raises. Let their work do the talking, pray, and trust God; and when the timing is right, they can ask to speak to their boss, without being demanding.

3 REASONS YOUR TEEN SHOULD QUIT A JOB

While I believe it is extremely important that we are steadfast and faithful in our work for an employer, there are times when you have very legitimate reasons to quit. Here are at least 3 of those reasons to explain to your teenager when the time may come.

1. Their job requires them to compromise their Christian principles. If their work is causing their walk with God to be compromised or diminished, it is probably time to quit. Perhaps it requires them to constantly miss church. Maybe they're being asked to do something that goes directly against their beliefs and values. If they trust God, He will lead them to something better.

2. Fellow employees are having a negative effect on their life. (2 Cor. 6:14.) The Bible instructs us not to be unequally yoked with unbelievers. If your child is becoming "yoked" together with an unbeliever on their job who is causing them to compromise or suffer temptation that is bringing them down, it's time to change jobs. The Bible says with temptation, God gives a way of escape. (1 Cor. 10:13.) It instructs us to "escape," not stay there and try to overcome it.

3. The Lord is leading them to something better. There are times when they may have a good job that is meeting their needs, but God has been preparing them for the next step—something even better. When a season

of faithfulness in one place comes to an end, encourage them to be obedient to step out to His next assignment for their life.

4 KINDS OF TEENS WHO CONSTANTLY GET FIRED

I have been in the workplace for more than 20 years and have never been fired from a job. Unfortunately, I have seen many others suffer this difficult experience. And many times teenagers don't make it on their jobs because of both a lack of experience and not being prepared for everything the workplace will bring. As parents, we must give them every chance to succeed. Many teens that end up getting fired fall into one of the following 4 categories.

1. Young people who cannot receive instruction or correction. Instead of acknowledging their shortcomings and making the appropriate changes, they overflow with pride and refuse to listen.

2. Those who cause strife in the team. A teenager may be a talented and diligent worker, but they allow jealousy, competitiveness, and hunger for power to sabotage their abilities.

3. Students who refuse to continue to grow and improve. Challenge your teen to never accept mediocrity and to be willing to pay the price to increase their knowledge and ability to perform at their highest level.

4. Those who are not truthful. No matter how talented a teenager is, they cannot help an organization if they cannot be trusted.

6 CAREERS YOUR TEEN CAN START RIGHT NOW

While youth is a time to have fun and enjoy life, it is also a time to learn the value of work and ambition. The Bible has much to say about the importance of working diligently.

Here are 6 careers that your son or daughter can embark on right now.

1. Newspaper business. Throw a paper route, and they will discover the satisfaction of getting a job done early.

2. Investment broker. There are companies that will take investment capital of just $50. They can learn how the market works and start investing a little at a time.

3. Graphic arts. If they have a bent for drawing and art, offer your assistance to find a place to use their gift. I know 14- and 15-year-olds who design logos and Web sites for companies and churches.

4. Film and video production. With an inexpensive camera and some software, they can be in the "movie" biz. My son began to be paid for his projects when he was just 15 years old.

5. Lawn care. If you have a mower and a weed-eater, have them distribute flyers in your neighborhood and sign up accounts to cut and trim grass after school and all summer.

6. Child care. Make their time available to families for quality baby-sitting services. Challenge them to be a good sitter, because they are hard to come by!

4 REASONS TEENS SHOULD GIVE AWAY
SOME OF WHAT THEY'VE WORKED FOR

When your teenager learns to work, God is going to bless them financially. If they want to continue to be blessed in good work opportunities, it is necessary to learn to give back out of their increase. Of course, we know that the Bible tells us to give a tithe (one-tenth) of our income to our local church, and offerings after the tithe to worthy causes. (Mal. 3:10,11.) There are at least 4 reasons your teenager will always have more after they give.

1. The Bible teaches that giving is like planting a seed. Every seed produces a huge multiplication of its kind. (2 Cor. 9:10.)

2. God promises to open heaven's windows and pour out blessings that they cannot possibly contain. (Mal. 3:10.)

3. Other people are naturally (and supernaturally) compelled to bless those who are unselfish in their giving. (Luke 6:38.)

4. Giving puts their faith in action, and faith is always rewarded abundantly by God. (Heb. 11:6.)

5 THINGS YOUR TEEN CAN DO WITH THEIR EARNINGS

Work will of course produce money, and money can take flight quickly if it is not put in a safe or productive place. Their work will be in vain if they are not wise with their earnings. An investment is something we contribute to without always seeing a quick or immediate return, trusting that its long-term results will be great.

Here are 5 investments your teenager can't afford not to make.

1. Invest in their church. The church is the vehicle by which the Gospel can go forth. Now is the time for them to commit to tithe.

2. Invest in missions. It would be great for them to find a person or ministry successfully reaching the lost and to help out by giving or going.

3. Invest in their financial future. Why not help them open a savings or money market account, and put something in it every month.

4. Invest in their career. Find their greatest interest in life (that can make them money), and put books in their hands that will help them succeed in that area.

5. Invest in their vocabulary. Words are powerful. Teach them new ones all the time, using them to be a better communicator, negotiator, and salesperson.

6 THINGS TEENS OUGHT TO KNOW ABOUT
MAKING GOOD MONEY

The Bible has literally hundreds of passages that discuss the issue of money. Next to God, it may well be the most powerful force in the earth. Your teen has got to know these 6 important things about making money.

1. It is not the root of all evil. Many say it is, but actually the Bible says, "The love of money is the root of all evil" (1 Tim. 6:10). That is a big difference.

2. No, it can't buy them love. It cannot purchase the love every human soul yearns for—the unconditional love of Jesus Christ.

3. They can have money and still be spiritual. The Bible commands Christians who are rich to be generous—not to take a vow of poverty. (1 Tim. 6:17-19.)

4. Money will come to those who work hard and plan carefully. (Prov. 21:5.)

5. Their good name and reputation for integrity are more important than a quick dollar. (Prov. 22:1.)

6. Don't seek money. Seek God and His wisdom. (Matt 6:33.) Solomon asked God for His wisdom, and everything else came to him!

3 THINGS MONEY WILL DO AND
3 THINGS MONEY WON'T DO FOR YOUR TEEN

Money can make many things happen for your son or daughter, but there are a few things that it cannot do. Learning to distinguish the difference may be one of the most important lessons they could ever learn.

Here are 3 things money can do for you.

1.   It can multiply. When they learn how to give and receive, buy and sell, invest and grow—money will multiply. (Luke 6:38.)

2.   It can be an instrument of love. When they use it to help the poor, the needy, or the lost, it becomes God's love in motion.

3.   It can be a testimony. As God has blessed and provided for them, when they give Him the glory, others will see God's goodness.

Here are 3 things money can't do for them.

1.   It can't soothe their conscience. Giving it away will never bring forgiveness of sin or relief of guilt. Only Christ can do that.

2.   It can't replace their work for God. Every Christian is called to actively serve in God's kingdom in some way. Just giving in the offering isn't enough.

3. It can't go to heaven with you. Don't hoard it. Have them make the best possible use of it while they're here!

5 THINGS A PARENT SHOULD TELL THEIR TEEN ABOUT WORK

Our work is very important to God. Unfortunately, there are a lot of teenagers who don't even think seriously about work until they get out of high school or even college, but now is the time to develop good work habits in their life. A strong work ethic will virtually ensure success in any career they choose.

Here are 5 critical things God's Word has to say about work.

1. If you don't work, you won't eat. (2 Thess. 3:10.) Work is the exchange God has created for all of us to gain finances to provide for our daily needs. God didn't say to pray, hope, or beg—He said to work.

2. We are to work as if our bosses were Jesus—not human beings. (Eph. 6:5.) Even when the boss isn't looking, the Lord sees all that you do.

3. Our work should produce good fruit and results. (Col. 1:10.) Don't just put in the time, but learn how to get results.

4. If we're faithful and consistent in the small things on our jobs, we'll be promoted to bigger tasks and responsibilities. (Matt. 25:23.)

5. A worker is worthy of one's pay. (Matt. 10:10.) You should be paid fairly for your work; and once you've agreed on a wage, you have no right to complain about your pay. Be cheerful!

7 PROMISES TO MAKE TO YOUR TEEN FOR DILIGENT WORK

Many young people seek to do the least they possibly have to at a job. What they fail to understand is that they are blocking the blessings of God from coming their way. Proverbs 21:5 assures us that the plans of the diligent will lead to plenty, while those who are hasty in their work will find poverty. Here are 7 promises any parent can make to their teen if they will dare to become a diligent worker.

1. Promotion. Hard work will be rewarded with higher positions of responsibility.

2. Recognition. A diligent person will stand out from the crowd, acknowledged by many.

3. Wealth. Companies and organizations will pay good money to those who do their job well.

4. Respect. They will gain esteem from friends, family, peers, and their community.

5. Opportunity. They will find themselves becoming very valuable to others who will open new doors for them to walk through.

6. Influence. They will earn the privilege of teaching, training, and mentoring those who will want to learn from their success.

7. Fulfillment. They'll never have to live with regrets, wondering what they could have accomplished if they had only given their best.

5 THINGS THAT WILL MAKE YOUR TEEN A VALUABLE EMPLOYEE

I currently have more than 20 full-time employees who serve under my direction and leadership. Each one of them is extremely important and valuable in contributing to our church and youth ministry. Here are the 5 qualities that make workers valuable.

1. Diligent. They give you 100 percent of their effort 100 percent of the time.

2. Smart. They think as they work, always coming up with better ways to get the job done more effectively.

3. Faithful. They will take just as much pride in and give as much attention to the small details of their work as they do big things.

4. Loyal. They speak well of you, fellow employees, and the organization to others and always seek what is best for the organization.

5. Productive. They get results, are careful with the finances, and help the organization grow.

[SECTION EIGHT:]

[SECTION EIGHT:]

what to do when your teen is almost done being a teen

4 WAYS TO HELP YOUR TEEN PURSUE A SCHOLARSHIP

With the ever-increasing cost of a college education, it is more important than ever to train your young person to work hard and smart for a possible scholarship. Few people have a bank account full of unlimited college funds, so here are a few tips to help you land the extra money you need for school.

1. Have them meet their school guidance counselor to help assess what kind of scholarships might be available. The sooner they can do this in their high school years, the more time they have to take those extra classes or join the extracurricular clubs that open more scholarship doors.

2. They have to hit the books. The better their grades, the more scholarship opportunities that will become available. If they pay the price now, they can have fun and play later, but if they choose to slack off and play now, it will cost them later.

3. Encourage them to stay involved in extracurricular activities. Colleges are looking for students who take the initiative and show signs of leadership.

4. Tell them to become an expert at something. I've met many students who have been given full scholarships because of their highly developed athletic ability. This didn't come just because they were talented, but because they were faithful to develop their gift every day. If they are not athletic, they may

be good in music, drama, or science. Look for a way for them to distinguish themselves. If they do, they may have schools fighting for your young person rather than you fighting for them.

4 THINGS TO THINK ABOUT WHEN IT COMES TO COLLEGE

Choosing what to do after high school can be a big decision. Is college the right thing, or should they start working? Maybe they need to mature a bit more and stay home and live off you for a little while longer.

Here are 4 things that will help you when considering your child's educational future.

1. A college education can open more doors of opportunity. Today, more and more employers are looking for college education as a qualification for even many entry-level positions. Without a degree many opportunities in medicine, law, finance, computers, and other professional fields can be very difficult to break into. This isn't to say they can't succeed without a degree, but it may be a much more difficult climb to the top.

2. Can they (you??) afford it? It can be very difficult to start life after college with a huge burden of school debt. Could they save money and still get the education they need by taking their first two years at a community college then transferring to an affordable university?

3. How will the school influence their spiritual life? Is this school known for its massive party atmosphere, or is it respected for its educational focus? Don't put them in a position to compromise by selecting the wrong school. Check the motives for wanting to attend a particular school.

4. Is there a good church they can attend while going to college? Without a good church their chances of a strong spiritual life are slim to none. If you put God first in choosing the right school, He will take care of adding everything to you. (Matt. 6:33.)

5 THINGS SCHOOL WON'T TEACH YOUR TEEN

Graduating from school isn't the end of learning—or at least it shouldn't be. School can teach your son or daughter many things about their chosen profession, but there are some very important things school will most likely never teach them. These things they must learn to pursue on their own.

1.   Living within their means. In today's society success doesn't have to be real as long as the clothes you wear, the house you live in, and the car you drive says you have reached the top of the success ladder. Many people are mortgaging their future by accumulating debt when they should be accumulating wealth. Challenge your teenager to delay instant gratification for true, long-term financial success.

2.   How to be happy with who they are. Today happiness is based on competition. Are they better looking than so-and-so, or are they better dressed, or is their car cooler? Don't allow your child to fall into this empty and vain comparison trap. Their happiness should be based on who they are in Christ and what He has created them to be.

3.   How to build a successful marriage. According to the National Center for Health Statistics, nearly half of all marriages end in divorce. As a parent, you don't want to spend months planning a wedding that lasts a few hours but spend no time preparing them to make their marriage last a lifetime.

Pass on books about building a marriage that will stand through the storms of life. Share the experiences you have had that can assist them in this important decision.

4. How to be a good parent. Most of us learned our parenting skills from how our parents raised us. This can be good, if we are doing a good job. Even then there are most likely things we would have done differently. Let them know those things in an honest way.

5. The meaning of life. The meaning of life can't be found in a school textbook. It can only be found in a personal relationship that your child has with their Creator. The closer they are to Him, the closer they will be to fulfilling their life's purpose.

4 WAYS TO UNLOCK YOUR TEEN'S LIFE ASSIGNMENT

Studies have proven again and again that people succeed most in doing what they love best. If we can accurately determine what we were created by God to do, we will truly find a life we will love living. Here are 4 ways to assist your child in unlocking the assignment God has on their life.

1. Show them how to delight in the Lord. (Ps. 37:4.) As they take joy in pursuing their personal relationship with Christ each day, the Bible promises that God will put His desires, drive, and passion in their life.

2. Challenge them not to be afraid to try new things. Take some risks. Try different kinds of activities, work, and projects. They may find something they're good at that no one knew about, including you.

3. Encourage them to ask for counsel from people they trust. (Prov. 11:14.) The Bible says in a multitude of counsel there is safety. As we ask those close to us that have a track record of success, God will use them to see the things we excel at most.

4. Spend regular time with them in prayer. You should also train them to pray on their own. (Jer. 33:3.) God told Jeremiah that if he would pray and call out to Him, that He would answer him, showing him great and mighty things that he knows not. The Hebrew meaning of that word *mighty* is

"hidden."[2] Prayer will unlock things in their life that could have remained hidden forever.

3 SUCCESS SECRETS YOUR TEEN MUST KNOW

There's not a teenager alive who doesn't want it—success—including yours. No one wants to go out and fail. Success should be every young person's goal, and God wants to help your teen attain it. But it is important that you define real success so that they know exactly what they're praying and preparing for.

1. Remind them that real success is never compared to someone else's achievements. Their measuring stick for success in life is not their big brother or best friend. Success for them is based on the talents God has given them and how well they develop and apply them.

2. Tell them that real success is loving God and loving people. All the money, power, and recognition in the world will not satisfy the deepest yearnings of the human soul. That's why many of the unhappiest people in the world are rich athletes, entertainers, and entrepreneurs. In the process of motivating them to reach their goals, urge them to love God and love people along the way.

3. Finally, real success is long term, not short term. (Matt. 16:26.) If they succeed by the world's standards for 70 or 80 years but pass from this life into eternity without God, what have they really gained? No one can afford to lose their soul while trying to gain in this world.

5 THINGS YOUR TEEN MUST DO TO GET A GREAT JOB

I've held a job since I was 12 years old. I've learned how to work hard and have never been fired. The sad thing is that along the way I've had to fire a lot of people. The thing that I've discovered is that if you give your best, you will have the opportunity to eventually do work that you enjoy and get promoted into a really cool job. Here are 5 ways to help your teen land a great job or career and keep it.

1. Motivate them to get out into the workplace and hunt their job down. Knock on doors, set up interviews, and learn to sell their skills and ability.

2. Be sure they have properly trained and prepared themselves for the job they really want. If it means college, find a way to get to college. Read, learn, intern, volunteer, and do whatever it takes to become the best in their field.

3. Tell them to be willing to start out in any company or organization. Be willing to do the small things that other "big shots" aren't willing to do. It will separate and distinguish them from the pack.

4. They must set their sights high. Don't allow their own self-doubt or other friends' lack of support stop them from going after their goals.

5. Pray and trust God together to open up the doors supernaturally. He can, and He will. (Mark 11:24.)

7 QUALITIES YOUR TEEN SHOULD LOOK FOR IN A FUTURE MATE

It's a good idea to know what your child really wants in a mate before they begin a relationship. If they wait until they're emotionally involved with someone, their judgment gets clouded and bad decisions are often the byproduct. Many young people wake up one day in a marriage they hate because they were not clear on what it was they really wanted. Aim at nothing and you will hit it every time. Here are 7 qualities your child should look for in a future mate.

1. **Equally yoked.** The apostle Paul warned us about being unequally yoked together with unbelievers. (2 Cor. 6:14.) Imagine being tied with a rope to another person while trying to run a race—you want to go west and they want to go east. How far will you get? It is important your son's or daughter's potential mate is going in the same direction spiritually that they are.

2. **Common interests.** It's good for them to have many of the same interests. It could be difficult if one person loves to be out often, is a world traveler, and likes meeting lots of people, but their spouse is content to stay home and is quiet and shy. They should both enjoy many of the same things.

3. **Same values.** Does this person have the same values your child has? Many relationships hit turbulent times because of sharp disagreements about values. They should talk about these before they get too involved.

4. **Like-minded goals.** Do they both want children? Do they want to be wealthy, or are they content to just get by? What are the goals for their life, marriage, family, and finances? They should be on the same page together.

5. **Respect.** It's a foundational stone for all healthy relationships. Does this person see your child's uniqueness and God-given gifts and treat them as special, or is this person spending all of his or her time trying to change them?

6. **Character.** Does this person have godly character? Does he or she do what is right, or what is popular and convenient? If you don't have character, you don't have anything.

7. **Attraction.** Your teenager should find this person attractive. Serving God and seeking Him first doesn't mean God is going to give your son or daughter a spouse they are not attracted to. The opposite is true. If they serve Him faithfully, He can get them one that is out of their league. He did for me. God wants them to have someone they love inside and out.

5 SIGNS THAT YOUR TEEN MAY BE READY TO MARRY

How do you know when your child is ready to get married? By society's standards it is being eighteen, having money for a wedding ceremony, and a willing fiancé. However, there should be much more than these if your child wants a marriage that will last a lifetime. Here are 5 indicators that they might be ready for marriage in the days ahead.

1.   They have a strong sense of self-esteem. The Bible says we are to love our neighbor as ourselves. (Matt. 22:39.) If they don't have a healthy love and respect for themselves, how can they genuinely love others? After all, love is the foundation for a good marriage.

2.   They are financially responsible. They must learn to be good with their money. Arguments over money is one of the top causes of divorce. Teach them not to spend every dime they make. Help them develop the discipline to save something each time they get paid; I suggest 10 percent.

3.   They have developed a good friendship with their potential mate. Marriage is about spending the rest of their life with their best friend. Marriages that are built on physical or romantic whirlwinds usually don't last. Friendship is the foundation for a love that lasts forever.

4. They and their potential spouse are in agreement about their values, dreams, and goals. Too often people spend all their time planning their wedding and honeymoon and never ask the real questions. Is this person I am about to marry going the same direction I am in life? Amos 3:3 asks the important question, "Can two walk together, unless they are agreed?"

5. They are prepared to live the rest of their life with this person just the way he or she is. Many people marry someone thinking they can change what they don't like about them after they get married. What if they never change? Can they live the rest of their life with their habits, quirks, and attitudes that drive them nuts? If it drives them nuts now, it will drive them insane later.

5 SECRETS TO PASS ON TO YOUR TEEN ABOUT
BUILDING RELATIONSHIPS

After graduation, your young person may move to a new school or a new job. A new place can often be intimidating and lonely. But it can also be a great adventure if your son or daughter learns how to take the initiative to meet new people. Even if they are naturally a shy person, if they follow these simple steps, they will find it easy to make new friends.

1. Take advantage of every opportunity to introduce themselves to people. It may be in the school bookstore, cafeteria, library, or a class. The more people they meet, the greater the odds they will find people they really connect with.

2. Remember to use people's names. There is no better sound to a person than his or her own name. If they aren't good at remembering names, here is a little trick that will help. When they introduce themselves and their new acquaintance gives them their name, they should be sure to use it right away. For example, "Fred, it sure is good to meet you. Fred, what classes do you have this semester?" If they can use their name at least three times in their conversation, they will be more likely to remember a name.

3. Teach them to ask questions about the lives of people they meet. Their conversation will be a hit because they are talking about everyone's favorite

subject—themselves! Everyone's favorite subject is themselves. It is often said, God gave us two ears and one mouth because He wants us to do twice as much listening as talking. A university study has found that good listening can be worth as much as 20 IQ points. I'll take all the extra points I can get!

4. Have good eye contact. If our eyes are always wandering during our conversation, people will feel we are uninterested in them. Also, poor eye contact can send them the message you are insecure or you are hiding something from.

5. They must be selective when choosing their closest friends. Close friends are people that influence our values, self-esteem, and dreams. Being careful to choose friends who love God like they do, believe in their dreams, and build them up is critical. If someone is always tearing your child down, they should do something about it—get some new friends. A famous mathematician once said, "You have to have seven positives to overcome one negative." Life is too short to waste it with people who don't believe in us.

7 THINGS YOUR TEEN SHOULD KNOW WHEN STARTING OVER

Everyone has felt the need to start over after making a mistake. You can help your teen if school's coming to an end and things didn't go as well as they should have. Here are some simple steps that will make starting over a success for your teenager.

1. Forgive themselves. When we confess our sins to God, He forgives and cleanses us. (1 John 1:9.) David wrote in Psalm 103:12 that "as far as the east is from the west, so far has He removed our transgressions from us." If God forgives and forgets our sins when we ask, we should also forgive ourselves. Jesus already took the punishment for our sin. Every teenager must learn to receive God's forgiveness by faith and get on with their life.

2. Learn from their mistake. Did they get into this bad situation because of poor decisions in their friendships, entertainment choices, or wrong priorities? If they can identify the root cause, then they can make changes to avoid this again in the future. Everyone makes mistakes, but to keep making the same one over and over is just plain stupid.

3. Focus on the future, not the past. Paul said, "...forgetting what is behind and straining toward what is ahead" (Phil. 3:13 NIV). Your teen can't successfully live in the present if they are always thinking about their past. Just because they can't rewrite yesterday doesn't mean they can't write a new story today.

4. Build healthy relationships. When starting over, it is good for your child to evaluate if they have the healthy relationships they need. Healthy relationships will give the emotional and moral support they need to change and build over. Proverbs 27:17 NIV says, "As iron sharpens iron, so one man sharpens another." They must pick their friends carefully. Look for ones that build them up and believe in them.

5. Set clear goals. Proverbs 29:18 KJV says, "Where there is no vision, the people perish." If we aim at nothing, we will hit it every time. Nothing great was ever achieved without vision.

6. Put goals in writing. The Bible tells us in Habakkuk 2:2, "Write the vision and make it plain on tablets, that he may run who reads it." Putting their vision in writing and making it clear will give them momentum to run toward their dreams. Maybe they want to lose 10 pounds, or retire wealthy, or become a black belt. Whatever their goals, encourage them to put them in writing and post them where they can see them every day.

7. Take steps. Many of their goals may be long term and seem hard to achieve. They don't have to take leaps towards dreams but rather simple steps. Proverbs 20:24 says, "A man's steps are of the Lord." You don't eat a steak in one big bite—you eat it one bite at a time.

3 REASONS TO ENCOURAGE YOUR TEEN TO BUY A HOUSE

The faster your teen can get in a position to buy their own house, the better. Help them understand that if they rent or lease, they are literally paying for someone else's home. Ten years later they may be out the door with nothing for their money, and their happy landlord has a house that's paid for and has increased in value. It's easier to buy a house today than they might think. Encourage them to talk to others that own a house and start doing some research. Meet with a good realtor. Here's why:

1. Property generally appreciates and goes up in value. Just about everything else they buy will go down in value—cars, jewelry, clothes—but a well-built home in a good area will usually be worth more in 5 years from now. It can become their first major investment vehicle.

2. They will build equity into their home over the length of the mortgage. Each month, a part of their mortgage payment is like cash they're putting into their own bank account. They are literally saving money every month. If they can afford to do a 15-year mortgage (higher payments) instead of a 30-year mortgage, they will save even more!

3. The United States government allows a housing deduction. They will save on their tax expenses each year as the government allows them to deduct their mortgage interest payments and property taxes from their federal income tax return. This is good news!

6 THINGS YOUR TEEN SHOULD KNOW ABOUT ROOMMATES

Your teen will have at least one roommate in life, and even if they don't, they will most likely get married. So, here are some good tips to pass on in regards to getting along with a roommate or spouse.

1.   Establish the house rules. Most arguments that occur are misunderstand-ings because the rules were not clearly defined. So sit down with them and write out the rules of the house. What are the rules about picking up after yourself, bringing guests over, cooking meals, the groceries, and the volume of the TV late at night?

2.   Respect each other's stuff. Most fights that occur are the result of not respecting each other's personal belongings or space. Don't use a room-mate's new sweater without permission or drink their last can of coke. Remember the golden rule of having a roommate and you will eliminate many arguments: "Do unto your roommate's stuff as you would have them do unto yours."

3.   Don't let frustrations build up. Jesus teaches us in Matthew to talk to those who offend us. (Matt. 18:15.) Rather than letting it build up or gossip to others about it, we must work it out with the person who offends us. Most of the time it was a simple misunderstanding and the relationship will become

stronger because it was dealt with. Relationships take work, lots of work, but they are worth it.

4. Prefer them above yourself. Paul wrote to the Philippians that we are to be like Christ and prefer others above ourselves. (Phil. 2:3-5.) Don't always think about what you want. Stop and think about the needs of your room-mate and put them above your own. If you do this, you will be amazed to see the difference it will make in the way your roommate treats you. According to Galatians 6:7, whatever a man sows, that is what he will reap.

5. Don't focus on the little things. It is amazing how most arguments happen over little things that make no difference in eternity, or even in this life for that matter. Stop, take a step back, and ask yourself if this will really matter a month from now or even at the end of the day.

6. Give them space for themselves. Everyone needs time to be alone. Respect your roommate's need for privacy. Before you have guests come over, call and see if it is okay. Little gestures of thoughtfulness like this will go a long way to building lasting friendships you can enjoy for years to come.

[SECTION NINE:]

[SECTION NINE:]

making your teen the influencer and not the influenced

4 DIFFERENCES BETWEEN GIVING YOUR TEEN
CONFIDENCE VS. ARROGANCE

Some people think that confidence is pride. You can be confident and very humble. Pride is confidence in the wrong things. True confidence comes from a solid foundation of knowing who you are in Christ. Look at these 4 differences between instilling confidence and arrogance in your young person.

1. Confidence is security in who they are in Christ. Arrogance is self-reliance because of what they have, who they know, or what they have done.

2. Confidence is knowing that they can do all things through Christ Jesus versus trusting what they can do on their own. (Phil. 4:13.)

3. Confidence is knowing their past is forgiven by God and they are in good standing with Him by faith. Arrogance is confidence in their works and their righteousness. (Eph. 2:8.)

4. Confidence is knowing that God is on their side, and therefore, it doesn't matter who is against them. Arrogance is security from circumstances and their own resources. (Rom. 8:31.)

Challenge them to be confident because of who they are in Christ Jesus. With Him on their side, they can't fail.

5 MARKS OF A CONFIDENT TEEN

Use this as a check to see if your teen is confident in who they are in Christ.

1. They aren't afraid to meet new people.

2. They like to try new things and see new places.

3. They aren't afraid to take calculated risks in order to achieve something they want.

4. They don't get discouraged and depressed when they fail. Instead, they pick themselves back up.

5. It doesn't bother them much when people criticize them.

If all of the statements above describe your teenager, they are very confident. If 4 of the statements are true about them, their confidence is solid and improving. Three true statements means they could use some improvement. It's not looking good if only 2 statements are true; they are limiting themselves from great experiences. If you found only 1 statement to be true, work with them in building their esteem and confidence every day until all the statements are true. Remember, in Christ they are a new creation. (2 Cor. 5:17.)

3 MUSTS FOR SUCCESSFULLY BUILDING
CONFIDENCE IN YOUR TEEN

If your young person needs more confidence in their life, here is a simple game plan that will help them grow.

1. Help them to find their identity in Christ Jesus. If they look to themselves for confidence, they will have many reasons to be insecure and disappointed. But in Christ, we are unlimited in our abilities. Look up these Scriptures: 2 Corinthians 5:17; Philippians 4:13; Colossians 1:22; Jude 24; Romans 8:15.

2. Surround them with people who believe in them as much as possible. Small people criticize big dreams. Don't allow their faith and self-esteem to be robbed by critical and negative people. Encourage people who speak into their life to build faith and strength with their words.

3. Help them take small steps to build big victories. We all have things in our lives we are secretly afraid of. Maybe it's heights, meeting new people, trying new foods, or sharing our faith. They don't have to take a huge leap of faith; just encourage them to take little steps towards overcoming their fears. The Bible says, "The steps of a good man are ordered by the Lord" (Ps. 37:23).

Build these 3 steps to confidence into their daily routine, and watch their confidence soar.

6 ENEMIES THAT WILL TRY TO STEAL ANY TEEN'S ABILITY TO INFLUENCE

In battle, one of the best advantages we can have is to understand our enemy. The more we know about our enemy, the better we can avoid his traps and attacks. Here are 6 enemies that will try to steal your son's or daughter's influence.

1. Negative people who criticize them. Assist them in choosing who their friends are. If their friends pull them down, it's time to get new friends.

2. Unconfessed sin. This will rob their confidence before God. Don't let them develop an Adam and Eve syndrome where they hide from God. Encourage them to go to Him, confess it, and be forgiven. (1 John 1:9.)

3. Listening to your feelings rather than God's Word. Feelings will betray them because they are subject to their circumstances. Fixing their eyes on God's unchanging Word is key.

4. Looking at their past to determine their future. They may have a past littered with failure, but that doesn't mean they can't succeed. A righteous person falls 7 times but keeps getting back up. (Prov. 24:16.)

5. Looking at the problem rather than God's promise for the solution. God's Word has a promise for any problem they face.

6. Comparing their life to the lives of other people. Tell them, "You are a great you but a lousy anyone else. Be you. You are great." (Jer. 1:5; 29:11; Ps. 138:8; 139.)

7 SCRIPTURES THAT WILL GIVE YOUR TEEN CONFIDENCE

Here are 7 encouraging Scriptures to help your young person look up and commit to memory.

1. Psalm 138:8: God will fulfill His purpose for their life.

2. John 3:16: God believed in them enough to allow His Son, Jesus, to die for them.

3. Mark 16:15: After Jesus rose from the dead, He gave His ministry to His disciples and them to finish.

4. Jude 24: He said He will keep them from falling and present them in His presence with great joy.

5. Acts 1:8: He gave them His power and Holy Spirit to witness.

6. John 15:16: He handpicked them. They're His first-round draft pick.

7. Ephesians 2:5: Even while we were lost, He made them alive with Him.

If God is confident in them, that should be all they need to know! He is the Creator of the universe, and He is on their side. They can't lose.

4 THINGS YOUR TEEN CAN DO TO GAIN INFLUENCE

The Bible encourages us in James 1:22 to be "doers of the word, and not hearers only." What your teenager says to others is important, but what they do will give them the right to say it. Here are 4 do's that we must encourage them to act on in order to influence those around them who do not know Jesus.

1. Do be generous. The Bible says in Proverbs 19:4 that a generous man has many friends. As they seek to help meet physical needs of people, they will eventually trust your young person with their spiritual needs as well.

2. Do live purely. If they have an immoral lifestyle, their words will fall on deaf ears. Their commitment to have pure relationships with people proves their testimony of a pure relationship with God.

3. Do be real. Have fun. Tell jokes. Enjoy life. Listen to music. Go to good movies. Play practical jokes. You get my drift. They shouldn't try to be so religious that they fail to relate to people. Remember, Jesus was criticized for hanging around sinners, yet kept Himself separate in His actions.

4. Do be patient. Have them think about all that God and people put up with in getting their life on track. They do not have the right to give up on anybody!

3 SIMPLE IDEAS YOUR TEEN CAN USE TO
REACH SOMEONE FOR CHRIST

Most people who have lost their way in America have heard many a preacher, either in church, on television or radio, or even on the streets of their city. They know they have sinned and come short of God's standard. It's going to take more than just more preaching. Jesus preached, but He also showed His love in practical ways. Here are some examples He set for us and our kids.

1. Jesus fed the multitude. Why? Because people need food to live, and because most people happen to like food! Your teen could ask a friend who doesn't know Christ out for dinner at a nice restaurant. It's neutral turf. A free meal. It's all good!

2. Jesus healed the sick. The Bible says those who believe will lay hands on the sick and they shall recover. (Mark 16:18.) The next time a friend, family member, or coworker complains about some kind of pain or discomfort, pray with your teen for them right away. Help them to see that we are not the healer but are simply inviting the Healer to bring His power into a life.

3. Jesus washed His disciples' feet. He came to serve, not to be served. What could your child do for someone they hope to influence for Christ? Help them in their yard? Clean their car? Assist them with homework?

Servanthood is one of the keys that opens the door of the Gospel in the lives of people.

3 STEREOTYPES YOUR TEEN MUST OVERCOME
AS A FOLLOWER OF CHRIST

Like it or not, as Christians we have to be prepared to overcome misperceptions that people in the world have about Christianity. Some of you may remember a popular sketch on "Saturday Night Live" that featured "The Church Lady," played by Dana Carvey. This judgmental character represented everything the world hates about religion and the church. Here are 3 common stereotypes your teenager can overcome by living out their faith in a real and genuine way.

1. "Christians think they're all perfect." We overcome this stereotype by being quick to acknowledge God's grace and forgiveness in our lives. Paul reminded the church that, of all sinners, he was chief! We must humbly acknowledge that without God's incredible mercy, we would all be lost.

2. "Christians think they know everything." We conquer this stereotype by simple being honest when we don't have an answer for someone. If your teen is talking about God with a friend and they bring up something they're not sure about, just admit they don't know the answer but will do some research and try to find out. Their not knowing everything about God doesn't make Him any less real!

3. "Christians don't have any fun." This one is easy. Tell your young person to have fun and enjoy life. Fun isn't getting drunk or high, or getting into bed

with a new person every weekend. Fun is having great friends who don't need artificial activities to enjoy life!

3 STEPS TO TEACH YOUR TEEN TO LEAD A FRIEND TO CHRIST

Winning people to Christ is one of the easiest things to do if we just know how. I've had the chance to do it hundreds of times. All it really takes is a gentle boldness, and once you do it once, it only gets easier. Here are 3 steps we can give to our kids in reaching out to their friends.

1. Cut to the chase and ask. At some point during their conversation with someone about God, stop everything and look them square in the eye and ask, "How would you like to be sure your sins are forgiven and know Jesus as your Lord and Savior?" More times than not, their answer will be, "Sure, I'd like to know that."

2. Stop everything and pray. Don't wait another second. Tell them that they can pray right now and make their heart right with God. Then they can lead the prayer and have their friend repeat: "Father in heaven, thank You for sending Jesus to die for my sins. I confess Jesus as my Lord and Savior. I believe He is alive and is coming to live in me now. Thank You for forgiving all my sins and giving me a brand-new heart, a heart that wants to please You. In Jesus' name. Amen."

3. Do their follow through. Get them to church. Show them in Scripture the importance of water baptism. Teach them how to read their Bible and pray.

This person is now a baby Christian and your young person will have to help them learn to walk.

5 THINGS TO EXPLAIN TO YOUR TEEN ABOUT SINNERS

Jesus said in Matthew 4:19, "Follow Me and I'll make you fishers of men." Good fishermen study all they can about how to successfully catch fish. They know what kind of bait to use, the right time of day, where in the lake to go, and the proper techniques needed to reel in the big one when it bites into the hook. We must be just as diligent and wise in our attempts to reach people. Here are 5 things your teen must know about a friend who does not know Christ in a personal way.

1. No matter how happy and confident they appear on the outside, deep inside they are empty and searching.

2. When they appear the most stubborn and hard towards the message, they are likely very close to breaking. Don't give up.

3. Their eyes can be opened to truth and the reality of God through your teenager's prayers.

4. Most of them already believe in God. They need someone to show them the next step.

5. They are caught better alone than in groups. Encourage your son or daughter to try to get with them one on one.

3 WAYS YOUR TEEN CAN LIFT SOMEONE UP

We grow up in a down world. Comedian Jerry Seinfeld pokes fun of parents who are always using the word "down" with their children. "Get down!" "Settle down." "Quiet down." "Turn that thing down!" You get the point. Many of the messages people hear in our world are not very positive. The nightly news is full of stories of war, crime, and tragedy. When your teenager has a message that encourages, they are sure to stand out from the crowd. Here are 3 messages they can share that will lift a person up.

1. "God created you to succeed in life." But like any created thing, you must find out exactly what you were created to do. A hammer isn't very good at being a screwdriver. But it's powerful when used for its creative purpose.

2. "No matter what you've done, Jesus Christ loves you without conditions." The Bible says that while we were yet sinners, Christ died for us. (Rom. 5:8.) When we were at our worst, Jesus gave us His very best.

3. "Heaven is a little like earth, without the bad days." The Bible talks about streets, trees, and rivers in heaven. So there are similarities to earth. Yet it promises no pain and no tears! It is absent of tragedy, depression, and temptation. And God has a mansion prepared for every one of His children. (John 14:2; Rev. 21:4, 21; Rev. 22:1, 2.)

3 WAYS YOUR TEEN CAN LIFT JESUS UP IN THEIR WORLD

How do we lift Jesus up in our world? Wear a big Christian T-shirt that says, "You're going to hell—ask me how!" Right? Well, maybe not. Not to say that the entire Christian T-shirt industry needs to shut down, but maybe just some of it. The world is looking for more of a witness than a cute little message printed on 100% cotton. There are real ways that your teenager can lift up Jesus in a real world. Here are a few.

1. Go the extra mile in all their work. Whether it's a job at McDonald's, early morning cheerleading or football practice, a biology class, or chores at home, give all they have and a little extra in all they do. This practice, when done consistently, will eventually provoke questions by curious observers, giving them the chance to share their reasons and faith.

2. Put a watch on their words. Guard their tongue, seeking to edify, encourage, and promote wholesome conversation. Refuse to gossip and betray the trust people have in their friendship. They will stand out from the crowd and will soon be given the chance to explain why.

3. Break out of their comfort zone. Help a stranger in need. Introduce themselves to a neighbor. Take a coworker out for lunch. Make a new friend. Each time they step into the life of someone else, incredible opportunities to share Christ are likely to follow.

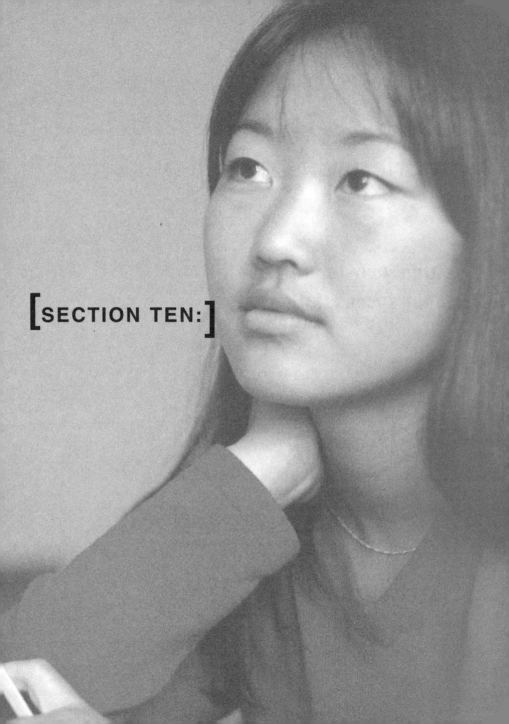

[SECTION TEN:]

[SECTION TEN:]

getting your teen through school successfully

4 THINGS YOUR TEEN NEEDS AT SCHOOL THAT NO ONE
WILL TEACH EXCEPT YOU

Make no mistake. Your child's teachers will give them important information that will prove valuable in the days to come: math, history, science, and trigonometry—okay, at least most of it will be valuable.

There are also some great things they'll need at school that their teachers aren't likely to teach that only you can. Here they are:

1. The art of discipline. Teach your teen to take advantage of their free time during or between classes to finish their assignments. This reduces homework!

2. How to negotiate. Develop their skills in learning how to work with teachers, coaches, and fellow students in the "give and take" of life in order to reach their goals.

3. Learn to say no. Classmates will ask them to cheat, lie, gossip, lust, vandalize—you name it. Help them put no in their vocabulary.

4. Love without respect of persons. They will meet people every day who don't appeal to them. Teach them to reach out to others with Christ's love in spite of their feelings.

7 WAYS TO HELP YOUR TEEN REMEMBER WHAT THEY STUDIED

When you think of school, you may think of tests. The key to your child passing is the ability to remember what they've learned a long time ago, even if they were only half awake and it was a Monday morning.

So here are some keys to helping them do just that.

1.   They must actually listen to the teacher while in class. Don't doze!

2.   Take good notes—even if their mind tells them they have the divine ability to "remember all things."

3.   Talk with them at the end of each day about what they've learned—even if it's spiced with a tinge of humor.

4.   Remind them about all the rewards that come with a good grade. (You do have rewards, don't you?)

5.   When studying, have them actually write their key points down again.

6.   When studying, they should say their key points aloud multiple times. We remember better what we hear ourselves say.

7. Pray with them and ask God together to bring those things they've learned back to their remembrance. (John 14:26.)

5 THINGS YOUR TEEN WILL WISH THEY'D LEARNED
10 YEARS AFTER GRADUATING

It's been more than 10 years since most of us as parents got out of high school and jumped into the "real world." Here's what I found out. No matter how bad you thought school was at the time, you will usually only remember the good times. Here are some things you should encourage your teenager to do before they graduate.

1. Keep a "highlights" journal. They don't have to write in it every day—just when cool things happen.

2. Take lots of pictures or video. It isn't just for them, but for their kids one day. The one thing my kids love to ask about is what I was like in high school.

3. Share their faith in Jesus with friends. They may think they'll be friends forever, but as you know, they won't. Some move away, others become too busy, some die, and others just drop right out. Challenge them to seize the day! (2 Cor. 6:2.)

4. Experiment. They should take a shot at different sports, new hobbies and interests, different classes, fresh challenges. They may catch on to something great you didn't know they could do!

5. Study hard and work hard. The discipline they develop today will bring the rewards you'll want them to enjoy a decade from now. (2 Tim. 2:15.)

4 WAYS TO HELP THEM MAKE SCHOOL GO BY QUICKLY

Why is it that when you're having fun, time seems to fly by, but when we were in school, it seemed like the clock had stopped or was even moving backwards? Simple: when you enjoy something, you don't care how long it takes.

Here are 4 ways your teenager can make school more enjoyable.

1. Set goals for their grades and achievement. If they develop a vision and stay focused on getting there, they'll move at a different pace. (Phil. 3:14.)

2. Have them create personal competitions in their classes and with their homework. As they work on each project, keep them motivated with a challenge of some kind. They can set themselves up against the clock, a previous grade, or even a fellow student.

3. Get involved in something at school they can really look forward to. It may be sports, a club activity, cheerleading, school council—in short, they should do something they like.

4. Go to school each day with a good mental attitude. Their mind and decisions control their emotions. Proverbs 23:7 NKJV says, "As he thinks in his heart, so is he." Decide every day, "This is the day the Lord has made. I will rejoice and be glad in it!" (Ps. 118:24.)

6 STUDENTS CLASSMATES LOVE TO HATE—
DON'T LET YOUR TEEN BE ONE OF THEM

A big part of enjoying school includes having friends your teenager looks forward to seeing every day. The Bible says that a person who wants friends must show oneself friendly. (Prov. 18:24.) Don't let your son's or daughter's attitudes and actions to cause them to be someone the other students hate to be around.

1.   The pity seeker feels sorry for him- or herself, trying to get the attention and pity of others.

2.   The bragger talks about him- or herself, what "I have," what "I can do," and what "I know."

3.   The loner isolates him- or herself from others, making it impossible for others to get to know them.

4.   The gossip always talks bad about others in the school, including those who are supposedly his or her friends.

5.   The roller-coaster goes up and down emotionally. One minute they are happy and a minute later they are crying.

6. The bully constantly demeans and picks one person that they perceive to be weaker than him- or herself.

3 REASONS YOUR TEEN'S MUSICAL INFLUENCES
ARE IMPORTANT

How many times have I heard teenagers tell me when referring to blatantly immoral messages in their music, "Well, Pastor Blaine, I don't listen to the words, so they don't affect me." I understand what they are trying to say, and I do believe you can make good choices in spite of listening to bad music. But there are 3 reasons good choices are critical for our teenagers as they are introduced to different kinds of music by friends at school.

1.   Messages, both good and evil, will have some effect on them. Why? Because the Bible teaches that there is power in words. Proverbs 23:7 teaches that as a man thinks in his heart, so is he. We are a product of our thoughts, and our thoughts are influenced by what we listen to in music or anything else.

2.   Their witness and testimony for Christ are on the line each day. If they are listening to music that is exalting fornication, murder, rebellion, etc., what does that say about their devotion to Christ to others around them?

3.   God's highest purpose for music is to facilitate worship and praise to Him in our lives. That's why an important part of the menu of music on their I-POD or in their CD case should be music that glorifies God and inspires them to serve Him.

4 DANGER ZONES IN YOUR TEEN'S ENTERTAINMENT

I enjoy good entertainment just as much as the next guy, but I believe that we all must guard the gates of our minds and hearts. Second Timothy 3:1-6 says we are to have nothing to do with wicked and ungodly people. This biblical principle also applies to your young person's entertainment.

Here are 4 danger zones that we should help them to steer clear of in modern entertainment.

1.   Sexual immorality. The Word of God says that there should not even be a hint of sexual immorality in our lives. (Eph. 5:3.) Encourage them to have the courage not to compromise even when everyone else does.

2.   Disrespect for authority. Honoring and obeying parents will bring them blessings. (Ex. 20:12.) Paul wrote that our police, military, and government leaders are ministers of God. (Rom. 13:6.)

3.   Mocking God. Do they realize that when they fail to react to others degrading God and godly principles, they come into agreement with those acts? Jesus said that if you're ashamed of Him and the Word, He will be ashamed of you. (Luke 9:26.)

4. Rage. They must reject the belief that uncontrolled anger will bring a solution to their problem. It won't. It will add to their already existing problems. Proverbs 14:16 NIV says, "A fool is hotheaded and reckless." Don't let them be a fool.

3 WAYS TO DEVELOP DISCERNMENT IN YOUR TEEN

I remember when I started out in the ministry as a youth evangelist back in the '80s. I did a "Rock Music Seminar," exposing a lot of the terrible lyrics that were in the music at that time. I played cuts off songs, had slides depicting evil-looking album covers—the whole deal! The problem was, I couldn't cover every teenager's music preferences in one night, and I was constantly having to update the seminar as new groups and artists were introduced and others faded. Rather than giving your teenager a list of the good, the bad, and the ugly, it would be better for you to teach them to discern what edifies and what doesn't for themselves. Here's how.

1. W.W.J.L.T. What would Jesus listen to? This is a great question to ask concerning anything in their music collection right now.

2. After listening to a certain group or artist, are they lifted up and inspired in all areas of life, including their faith in God?

3. The Word of God and the Holy Spirit. Is what they are listening to contradicting what God's Word teaches, and is the Holy Spirit grieved by any of their choices?

5 WAYS YOUR TEEN CAN HAVE A GREAT TIME
WITHOUT COMPROMISING

"Christians don't have any fun." That's the worst lie that's ever been pushed on young people in today's world! I've been a Christian since I was 16 years old, and I've had the time of my life the whole way. Give your teenager 5 ways to get their life on the fast track.

1. Reach out and make some great friends with similar interests. Good friends can be a blast to hang out with. Laughing, talking, going places, learning how to live life together—it's awesome!

2. Find a hobby or activity they love. It may be a sport, collecting something, hunting, writing, acting, dancing—whatever. Just do something that they can look forward to.

3. Learn how to throw a great party without drugs, alcohol, and sex. A lot of Christian parties are boring because nothing is planned. It might be a great new game, karaoke, cooking everyone's favorite dish—just be creative!

4. Get into trouble that doesn't hurt anyone. It might be a great practical joke they and their friends play on somebody. Don't get me started. I love doing stuff like this!

5. Make a list of things they've never done or tried and want to do. Big stuff.
Cool stuff. Now start making plans to check off everything on their list.

5 SCRIPTURES TO GUIDE YOUR TEEN'S

DAILY ENTERTAINMENT CHOICES

In evaluating things we watch, listen to, or do, it is important to allow God to help your teen with decisions by comparing their choices to God's instruction. Believe it or not, the Bible has a lot to say about entertainment. Here are 5 awesome Scriptures to use in all their evaluations.

1. "Finally, brethren, whatever things are true, whatever things are noble, whatever things are just, whatever things are pure, whatever things are lovely, whatever things are of good report, if there is any virtue and if there is anything praiseworthy—meditate on these things" (Phil. 4:8). What kind of thoughts is this producing in their life?

2. "And do not be conformed to this world, but be transformed by the renewing of your mind, that you may prove what is that good and acceptable and perfect will of God" (Rom. 12:2). Is this causing them to conform to a worldly attitude or behavior?

3. "According to the eternal purpose which He accomplished in Christ Jesus our Lord" (Eph. 3:11). Does it fall in line with God's purpose for their life?

4. "It is better to hear the rebuke of the wise, than for a man to hear the song of fools" (Eccl. 7:5). The Bible says a fool says, "There is no God." Is their entertainment denying the existence or goodness of God?

5. "And the tongue is a fire, a world of iniquity. The tongue is so set among our members that it defiles the whole body, and sets on fire the course of nature; and it is set on fire by hell" (James 3:6). The tongue has power to destroy with the words it speaks. What kind of words are they allowing into their spirit?

7 GUARANTEES YOUR TEEN HAS FOR TRUE FRIENDSHIPS

God recognized man's need for relationship when He created a companion for Adam in the Garden of Eden. In Genesis 2:18, God said, "It is not good that man should be alone." Our teens need godly relationships in their lives to strengthen and encourage them. Here are 7 Bible guarantees for friendship in their life.

1.   God's Word guarantees that they will have friends if they show themselves friendly. Proverbs 18:24 says, "A man who has friends must himself be friendly." The Bible encourages us to take the first step and initiate friendships. They will have quality friends if they make the effort to always be friendly.

2.   God's Word guarantees that godly friends make them stronger. Proverbs 27:17 says, "As iron sharpens iron, so a man sharpens the countenance of his friend." Good friends will sharpen them, because they are moving in the same direction.

3.   God's Word guarantees that godly friends will help them realize their potential. Proverbs 20:5 says, "Counsel in the heart of man is like deep water, but a man of understanding will draw it out." God has a unique purpose for your teen. Good friendships will help them achieve all that God has planned for their future.

4. God's Word guarantees that true friends will stick with them no matter what. Proverbs 17:17 says, "A friend loves at all times, and a brother is born for adversity." Fair weather friends will leave at the first sign of trouble. But true friends do not change their attitude towards us just because negative circumstances arise.

5. God's Word guarantees that they will become wise if they hang out with wise friends. Proverbs 13:20 says, "He who walks with wise men will be wise…." Friendships influence almost all of our choices. If they surround themselves with wise friends, they will learn to make wise choices in every area of life.

6. God's Word guarantees that they can avoid suffering by not hanging out with foolish people. Proverbs 13:20 says, "…But the companion of fools will be destroyed." This verse warns that if they choose to hang out with foolish friends, they will share the same fate.

7. God's Word guarantees that they will reap what they sow into their friendships. Galatians 6:7 says, "…whatever a man sows, that he will also reap." If they spend time developing strong relationships, those relationships can become a great resource. Friendships have to be nurtured in order to thrive.

5 ATTITUDES THAT WILL MAKE YOUR TEEN A FRIEND MAGNET

There are always those people that you are naturally attracted to, those friends that you want to spend all of your free time with. What is it about those people that makes others want to be around them? Here are 5 character traits that make young people friend magnets.

1. Happy. Nobody wants to be around a grump. A great attitude is one of the strongest magnets for friends. When your teen is happy, it's contagious. They should always try to stay upbeat, and they will never cease to be in the company of friends.

2. Encouraging. Choosing to lift other people up with a kind word or a generous action will naturally draw other people to their side. A word in due season is often just the encouragement someone else needs. (Prov. 15:23.)

3. Generous. Unselfishness has a powerfully attractive force. By choosing to share and think of others before themselves, they show people that they value them.

4. Objective. It's nice to be around people who are willing to hear the opinions of others. Let's face it, they're not always right, so they must pick their battles carefully and be willing to accept someone else's idea if it's better than theirs.

5. Helpful. They're not much of a friend if they're not willing to lend a hand. It works both ways. There will be a time when they need some help, so sow the seeds of friendship now, and reap the rewards later.

ENDNOTES

[1] *Webster's New World Dictionary,* 3d Edition. New York: McMillian Company, s.v. "channel."

[2] *Matthew Henry's Commentary on the Whole Bible,* Volume 1, Hendrickson Publishers, s.v. "mighty."

PRAYER OF SALVATION

God loves you—no matter who you are, no matter what your past. God loves you so much that He gave His one and only begotten Son for you. The Bible tells us that "…whoever believes in him shall not perish but have eternal life" (John 3:16 NIV). Jesus laid down His life and rose again so that we could spend eternity with Him in heaven and experience His absolute best on earth. If you would like to receive Jesus into your life, say the following prayer out loud and mean it from your heart.

Heavenly Father, I come to You admitting that I am a sinner. Right now, I choose to turn away from sin, and I ask You to cleanse me of all unrighteousness. I believe that Your Son, Jesus, died on the cross to take away my sins. I also believe that He rose again from the dead so that I might be forgiven of my sins and made righteous through faith in Him. I call upon the name of Jesus Christ to be the Savior and Lord of my life. Jesus, I choose to follow You and ask that You fill me with the power of the Holy Spirit. I declare that right now I am a child of God. I am free from sin and full of the righteousness of God. I am saved in Jesus' name. Amen.

If you prayed this prayer to receive Jesus Christ as your Savior for the first time, please contact us on the Web at **www.harrisonhouse.com** to receive a free book.

Or you may write to us at:

Harrison House
P.O. Box 35035
Tulsa, Oklahoma 74153

MEET BLAINE BARTEL

 Blaine Bartel is one of America's premiere leadership specialists. Blaine served as Oneighty®'s Youth Pastor for 7 years, helping it become America's largest local church youth ministry, reaching more than 2,500 students each week. He is now the National Director of Oneighty® and Associate Pastor of 12,000-member Church On The Move in Tulsa, Oklahoma. Blaine has served under his Pastor and mentor, Willie George, for more than 20 years. God has uniquely gifted him to teach local church staff and workers to thrive while faithfully serving the vision of their leader. Known for his creativity and respected for his achievement, Blaine uses the Thrive audio resource to equip thousands of church and youth leaders each month with principles, ideas, and strategies that work.

past: Came to Christ at age 16 on the heels of the Jesus movement. While in pursuit of a professional freestyle skiing career, answered God's call to reach young people. Developed and hosted groundbreaking television series, *Fire by Nite.* Planted and pastored a growing church in Colorado Springs.

passion: Summed up in three simple words, "Serving America's Future." Blaine's life quest is "to relevantly introduce the person of Jesus Christ to each new generation of young people, leaving footprints for future leaders to follow."

personal: Still madly in love with his wife and partner of 23 years, Cathy. Raising 3 boys who love God: Jeremy—19, Dillon—17, Brock—15. Avid hockey player and fan, with a rather impressive Gretzky memorabilia collection.

To contact Blaine Bartel,

please write to:

Blaine Bartel

Serving America's Future

P.O. Box 691923

Tulsa, OK 74169

E-mail: bbartel@churchonthemove.com

Or visit him on his Web site at:

www.blainebartel.com

To contact Oneighty®,

please write to:

Oneighty®

P.O. Box 770

Tulsa, OK 74101

www.Oneighty.com

OTHER BOOKS BY BLAINE BARTEL

Ten Rules to Youth Ministry and Why Oneighty®
Breaks Them All

Oneighty® Devotional

every teenager's
little black book
on reaching your dreams

every teenager's
little black book
of God's guarantees

every teenager's
little black book
on how to get along with your parents

every teenager's
little black book
for athletes

every teenager's
little black book
on how to win a friend to Christ

every teenager's
little black book
on sex and dating

every teenager's
little black book
on cash

every teenager's
little black book
on cool

every teenager's
little black book
of hard to find information

little black book
for graduates

for more information on the
little black book series,
please visit our Web site at:
www.littleblackbooks.info

additional copies of this book
are available from your local bookstore.

Harrison House
Tulsa, Oklahoma

DO THE EVOLUTION.

No, not the monkey thing. Evolution is change—steady, consistent, everyday change. Are you ready for a Oneighty® in your life? Then take the challenge. Give God five minutes of your day and watch the change begin.

The Oneighty® Devotional is as simple as 1-8-0. Study "1" Scripture a day. Commit to "8" weeks. Take the "0" pledge.

When you complete the *Oneighty® Devotional,* the Word of God will be more real and alive to you than ever before. Your mind will be renewed, and you will experience a 180-degree turn that will change your relationships, your prayer life, your self-esteem, and every other area of your life.

www.harrisonhouse.com

Fast. Easy. Convenient!

◆ New Book Information ◆ Free E-News
◆ Look Inside the Book ◆ Author Biographies
◆ Press Releases ◆ Upcoming Books
◆ Bestsellers ◆ Share Your Testimony

For the latest in book news and author information, please visit us on the Web at www.harrisonhouse.com. Get up-to-date pictures and details on all our powerful and life-changing products. Sign up for our e-mail newsletter, *Friends of the House,* and receive free monthly information on our authors and products including testimonials, author announcements, and more!

Harrison House—
Books That Bring Hope, Books That Bring Change

THE HARRISON HOUSE VISION

Proclaiming the truth and the power

Of the Gospel of Jesus Christ

With excellence;

Challenging Christians to

Live victoriously,

Grow spiritually,

Know God intimately.